*This*
PRAYER JOURNAL
*belongs to*

......................................................................................................

# A YEAR OF GOD'S *Goodness*

A

PRAYER & PRAISE TRACKER

*for* WOMEN

BARBOUR
PUBLISHING

ISBN 979-8-89151-039-5

Text previously appeared in *365 Moments of God's Goodness*, published by Barbour Publishing, Inc.

Cover Design: Greg Jackson, Thinkpen Design

Published by Barbour Publishing, Inc., 1810 Barbour Drive, Uhrichsville, Ohio 44683, www.barbourbooks.com

*Our mission is to inspire the world with the life-changing message of the Bible.*

Member of the
Evangelical Christian
Publishers Association

Printed in China.

*Taste and see that the LORD is good.*
*Oh, the joys of those who take refuge in him!*

PSALM 34:8 NLT

The goodness of God is all around. If we take the time to look, we'll see it in the dawn of a new day's sun. We'll discover it in a conversation with a friend. We'll see it in the commute to school or work. We'll find it in the miraculous and in the mundane; in the challenges and in the triumphs; in the joys and in the unexpected reminders of God's love for us.

Because in all things God *is* good.

What better way to spend the next year than with a tool that can help your prayer life flourish? That's just what this book can do.

Part daily devotional, part prayer journal, and part prayer tracker, this fantastic guide gives you everything you need to spend a few minutes every day in prayer. Each day includes a scripture, quote, or encouraging thought, and a short devotional prayer. Below that, you'll be able to write down what's on your own heart in a conversation with God. Don't worry about making your prayer perfect or even eloquent. The Bible tells us in Jeremiah 29:12 that when we talk to God, He is faithful to listen to us. At the bottom of the page are dedicated spots for your prayer requests, praises, and answers to prayer.

At the end of the year, this journal will serve as a beautiful reminder of the daily goodness God gave you. His goodness is always there. . .we just have to notice it. . .and be blessed!

## *Day 1*
# LOOK FORWARD

Instead of feeling sorry for ourselves as we advance in years or toting up the days and months that are already past, let's praise God for all the benefits He's already given and look forward to all those that may lie ahead.

*As I look back on my life, Lord, remind me that Your plans for me are good. Thank You for the joy from days gone by, but You're not finished with me yet. I have much to look forward to because I continue to live my life fully surrendered to You.*

PRAYER REQUESTS

PRAISES

ANSWERS TO PRAYER

# Day 2

## HIS PERFECT PLAN

Every experience God gives us, every person He puts in our lives,
is the perfect preparation for the future that only He can see.
CORRIE TEN BOOM

*Dear Lord, sometimes I feel like I missed You. But I take courage today because You have set a path before me. I will not miss the mark. Help me to use my experiences to grow in faith and point others to You.*

| PRAISES |
|---|
| |

| PRAYER REQUESTS |
|---|
| |

| ANSWERS TO PRAYER |
|---|
| |

*Day 3*
# THE BEST THINGS

The best things are nearest: breath in your nostrils, light in your eyes,
flowers at your feet, duties at your hand, the path of God just before you.
Do not grasp at the stars, but do life's plain common work as it comes,
certain that daily duties and daily bread are the sweetest things of life.
ROBERT LOUIS STEVENSON

*Heavenly Father, You are good, and all that You have created is good. Forgive
me when I take the small things for granted. Today I count my blessings and
give You thanks for the little things. Thank You for giving me the gift of life.*

## PRAYER REQUESTS

## PRAISES

## ANSWERS TO PRAYER

## *Day 4*
# SPIRITUAL BLESSINGS

Let us honor and thank the God and Father of our Lord Jesus
Christ. He has already given us a taste of what heaven is like.
EPHESIANS 1:3 NLV

*I praise You, God, for the gift of eternal life and the opportunity to
spend eternity with You. Lord, help me to see heaven in the little things
here on earth. Thank You for a taste of heaven on earth.*

PRAISES

PRAYER REQUESTS

ANSWERS TO PRAYER

## Day 5
# UNBELIEVABLE FAITH

In the present state of things, [faith] is the only means under heaven for
effecting [the law of love]; it is on that account an unspeakable blessing to man.

JOHN WESLEY

*Thank You for Your unconditional, unmerited love. Give me the faith to receive Your love
even when I don't feel it. I trust You, God, to always be with me, giving me the ability
to live my very best life in Your strength because You love me! Your love never fails.*

_____

## PRAYER REQUESTS

_____

## ANSWERS TO PRAYER

_____

## PRAISES

_____

## Day 6

# BEAUTIFUL DAWN

How beautiful it is to be alive! To wake each morn as if the Maker's
grace did us afresh from nothingness derive, that we might sing
"How happy is our case! How beautiful it is to be alive!"
HENRY SEPTIMUS SUTTON

*Each day is a gift. Every day that I have breath is a day You've given me to do
Your will, to give You praise, and to point others to You. Thank You for Your
grace that makes each day more precious because I can spend it with You.*

.................................................................................
.................................................................................
.................................................................................
.................................................................................
.................................................................................

## PRAISES

## PRAYER REQUESTS

## ANSWERS TO PRAYER

# *Day 7*
## HE LONGS TO LISTEN

Isn't it great that God wants us to talk to Him about all our worries and cares? What a gift that He cares about everything that happens to us every step of the way.

*You are my own audience of one. You always hear me. You are concerned about the things that are important to me. No matter how small the issue, You are always genuinely interested. Praise to You, Father, for being willing to listen to me.*

### PRAYER REQUESTS

### ANSWERS TO PRAYER

### PRAISES

*Day 8*

# THE BEST IS YET TO COME

Our heavenly Father never takes anything from His children
unless He means to give them something better.
GEORGE MÜLLER

~

*When I am discouraged or disappointed, I look to You, Lord. Whatever I feel I've missed,*
*I know You have something better. You have laid out a path for my life, and I will not*
*miss Your goodness. You always have something better because the best is yet to come!*

## PRAISES

## PRAYER REQUESTS

## ANSWERS TO PRAYER

## Day 9
# HOW REFRESHING!

The beauty and loveliness of all other things are fading and
perishing, but the loveliness of Christ is fresh for all eternity.
JOHN FLAVEL

*Like a gentle rain softly pitter-pattering on my head, Your peaceful presence brings a
beauty that cannot be measured with all of creation. Pour Your presence out on me
in a fresh and new way. Help me to see Your beauty in the things You do in my life.*

......................................................................................................................................
......................................................................................................................................
......................................................................................................................................
......................................................................................................................................
......................................................................................................................................
......................................................................................................................................

### PRAYER REQUESTS

......................................................................
......................................................................
......................................................................
......................................................................

### PRAISES

......................................................................
......................................................................
......................................................................
......................................................................
......................................................................
......................................................................
......................................................................
......................................................................
......................................................................
......................................................................
......................................................................

### ANSWERS TO PRAYER

......................................................................
......................................................................
......................................................................
......................................................................

# *Day 10*

# DIVINE PROVIDENCE

You will eat the fruit of your labor; blessings and prosperity will be yours. Your wife will be like a fruitful vine within your house; your children will be like olive shoots around your table. Yes, this will be the blessing for the man who fears the LORD.

PSALM 128:2–4 NIV

*Thank You for my beautiful family. You bless them in all they do. You lead, guide, and protect them in all they do wherever they go. I revere and honor You, Lord. Thank You for helping me to be a blessing to them. Help me to lead my family according to Your plan.*

## PRAISES

## PRAYER REQUESTS

## ANSWERS TO PRAYER

# *Day 11*
# ETERNAL GRATITUDE

*Lord, thank You for every blessing, both big and small. Help me to be more aware of the ways in which You take care of me, so my gratitude can continue to grow. Remind me that everything good in this lifetime and for all of eternity comes from You. May I never take anything for granted—my health, my provision, my family and friends, or my relationship with You. When things are hard, help me to use it to grow closer to You. Amen.*

## PRAYER REQUESTS

## ANSWERS TO PRAYER

## PRAISES

*Day 12*

# BE PREPARED

Above all else, know this: Be prepared at all times for the gifts of
God and be ready always for new ones. For God is a thousand
times more ready to give than we are to receive.

MEISTER ECKHART

*God, You are a giver. That's what You do! Thank You for all You've given me. Help me
to be prepared at all times, ready to receive whatever gifts You have for me with gratitude and an obedient heart. I will use them to bring You pleasure without complaint.*

## PRAISES

## PRAYER REQUESTS

## ANSWERS TO PRAYER

## *Day 13*
# WONDERFUL PLANS

God is still in control of every situation. The universe belongs to Him, including all the people in it. At such a time as this, He may be planning something wonderful, a mere step beyond the problem we face. Just because we don't see the blessing yet doesn't mean it isn't on its way.

*You are a big God! I know You do miracles. Open my eyes to see Your handiwork. And when I can't see what You are doing, increase my faith to trust that all things work together for my good because I love You. The blessings are already on the way.*

........................................................................................................................................
........................................................................................................................................
........................................................................................................................................
........................................................................................................................................
........................................................................................................................................

### PRAYER REQUESTS
........................................................................
........................................................................
........................................................................
........................................................................

### PRAISES
........................................................
........................................................
........................................................
........................................................
........................................................
........................................................
........................................................
........................................................
........................................................
........................................................

### ANSWERS TO PRAYER
........................................................................
........................................................................
........................................................................
........................................................................

## *Day 14*
# SIMPLE THINGS

Into all our lives, in many simple, familiar, homely ways,
God infuses this element of joy from the surprises of life,
which unexpectedly brighten our days and fill our eyes with light.

Samuel Longfellow

*God, You are always surprising me. Forgive me when I don't respond well to
the unexpected gifts You give me. I am grateful for the joy that comes because of
Your plans for my life. You are the light of my life, where my joy comes from!*

## PRAISES

## PRAYER REQUESTS

## ANSWERS TO PRAYER

*Day 15*

# HEART GIFTS

It's not the things that can be bought that are life's richest treasure,
It's just the little "heart gifts" that money cannot measure.
A cheerful smile, a friendly word, a sympathetic nod,
Are priceless little treasures from the storehouse of our God.

HELEN STEINER RICE

*Thank You for the little things. I never want to discount the treasures You bestow upon me. As I go about my day, help me to slow down to see the little gifts You have sent my way. May I also show kindness and be Your gift to others.*

......................................................................................................................................
......................................................................................................................................
......................................................................................................................................
......................................................................................................................................
......................................................................................................................................

## PRAYER REQUESTS

......................................................................
......................................................................
......................................................................
......................................................................

## PRAISES

......................................................................
......................................................................
......................................................................
......................................................................
......................................................................
......................................................................
......................................................................
......................................................................
......................................................................

## ANSWERS TO PRAYER

......................................................................
......................................................................
......................................................................
......................................................................

## *Day 16*
# BLESSINGS ALWAYS

"I will make you into a great nation, and I will bless you; I will make your name great, and you will be a blessing. I will bless those who bless you, and whoever curses you I will curse; and all peoples on earth will be blessed through you."

GENESIS 12:2–3 NIV

*Thank You, Father, for adopting me into Your family and blessing me. May I always remember that because I belong to You, Your blessing belongs to me. You give good gifts to Your children. Let my faith rise to believe that good things are on the way.*

### PRAISES

### PRAYER REQUESTS

### ANSWERS TO PRAYER

## *Day 17*
# INSTANT COMFORT

Faith is the root of all blessings. Believe, and you shall be saved; believe,
and you must needs be satisfied; believe, and you cannot but be comforted.

JEREMY TAYLOR

*God, I believe Your Word. I have faith that it is true. Thank You for Your promise to
comfort and keep me in all my ways. Assign Your angels today to go before me and
behind me, always providing a way of escape when I am trapped or tempted.*

## PRAYER REQUESTS

## PRAISES

## ANSWERS TO PRAYER

## *Day 18*

# LIFE-CHANGING REALIZATION

Count your blessings. Once you realize how valuable you are and how much you have going for you, the smiles will return, the sun will break out, the music will play, and you will finally be able to move forward in the life that God intended for you with grace, strength, courage, and confidence.

OG MANDINO

*Today I count my blessings. I have breath in my lungs, strength in my body, presence of mind. You have given me food on my table. I lack no good thing because I belong to You. As Your child, I am precious and valuable. I am the apple of Your eye.*

## PRAISES

## PRAYER REQUESTS

## ANSWERS TO PRAYER

# Day 19
## THE CYCLE OF JOY

When we've made it our lifestyle to take hold of God's Word and teachings and use them to show others how to live, we are truly blessed—and so are others who come in contact with us. Their growth in turn touches others' lives—and on and on it goes. The joys of mercy, peace, and love abound, just as God planned.

*Thank You for Your Word. It is a light to my path and a lamp to my soul. Your words give me courage, strength, and hope for tomorrow. Please help me to choose each day to live my life in a way that honors You and points others to choose You.*

### PRAYER REQUESTS

### PRAISES

### ANSWERS TO PRAYER

## Day 20
# OPEN YOUR EYES

I have often thought it would be a blessing if each human being were stricken blind and deaf for a few days at some time during his early adult life. Darkness would make him more appreciative of sight; silence would teach him the joys of sound.

HELEN KELLER

*I never want to be ungrateful for anything You've given me. Show me, Lord, anything in my heart that I take for granted, from the air I breathe to the people you have placed in my life. All I have is given to me from You. Teach me to appreciate everything in my life.*

## PRAISES

## PRAYER REQUESTS

## ANSWERS TO PRAYER

## *Day 21*
# HIDDEN BLESSINGS

God left the world unfinished. . .the pictures unpainted and the music unsung and
the problems unsolved, that man might know the joys and glories of creation.
THOMAS S. MONSON

*When I look at creation, God, I see You. I look at new life and wonder how anyone
could not believe in You. Thank You for the opportunity to be alive today and be a
part of Your plan. Help me to be faithful to complete the work You've set before me.*

## PRAYER REQUESTS

## PRAISES

## ANSWERS TO PRAYER

# *Day 22*
# GIVING

"Give, and it will be given to you. A good measure, pressed down,
shaken together and running over, will be poured into your lap.
For with the measure you use, it will be measured to you."
LUKE 6:38 NIV

*Father, I want to be generous! But sometimes it's hard not to hold on to what I have for
fear that it might be lost. Forgive me. Help me to hold all things loosely. Show me how
I can give to others so that they see Your light in me. I realize I can never outgive You.*

## PRAISES

## PRAYER REQUESTS

## ANSWERS TO PRAYER

# *Day 23*
## SEEK HIS GUIDANCE

*Lord, You've given me a life that abounds in rich blessings, and You've guaranteed that because of this, You also have great expectations of me. Help me to be faithful to these expectations. If I consider them without applying faith, they are overwhelming. But You never asked me to do anything without Your help. Faith is the substance of things hoped for. I put my hope in You to bring these expectations to reality.*

......................................................................................................................................

......................................................................................................................................

......................................................................................................................................

......................................................................................................................................

......................................................................................................................................

......................................................................................................................................

......................................................................................................................................

### PRAYER REQUESTS

......................................................................................

......................................................................................

......................................................................................

......................................................................................

### ANSWERS TO PRAYER

......................................................................................

......................................................................................

......................................................................................

......................................................................................

### PRAISES

......................................................................................

......................................................................................

......................................................................................

......................................................................................

......................................................................................

......................................................................................

......................................................................................

......................................................................................

......................................................................................

......................................................................................

# Day 24
## SEASONAL BLESSINGS

The four seasons. . .demonstrate creation's thankfulness to God for a job
well done. The trees bow before heaven as their leaves fall gracefully
to the ground. The glistening snowfall speaks of God's majesty.
Flowers of every kind bow low to the glory of God in spring, and
summer warms to the glow of all the blessings God has to offer.

*Life becomes so busy, I can hardly lift my head from the tasks. But I will look up
to You. You created this world, and Your majesty is all around. Remind me to
enjoy the world You created for me to enjoy. May I see You everywhere I look.*

### PRAISES

### PRAYER REQUESTS

### ANSWERS TO PRAYER

## *Day 25*
# ONLY ONE

Most of all the other beautiful things in life come by twos and threes, by
dozens and hundreds. Plenty of roses, stars, sunsets, rainbows, brothers
and sisters, aunts and cousins, but only one mother in the whole world.

KATE DOUGLAS WIGGIN

*Thank You, Lord, for my mother. You chose her to be my mother. Your Word says to
honor my mother, and I do so right now. Bless her, Lord! May she know and love You all
the days of her life. Remind me to bless her with my words and to show her Your love.*

.......................................................................................................................................................
.......................................................................................................................................................
.......................................................................................................................................................
.......................................................................................................................................................
.......................................................................................................................................................

### PRAYER REQUESTS

.........................................................................
.........................................................................
.........................................................................
.........................................................................

### ANSWERS TO PRAYER

.........................................................................
.........................................................................
.........................................................................
.........................................................................

### PRAISES

.........................................................................
.........................................................................
.........................................................................
.........................................................................
.........................................................................
.........................................................................
.........................................................................
.........................................................................
.........................................................................
.........................................................................
.........................................................................

## Day 26
# BEARABLE BURDENS

*Lord, we sometimes sing a song about being happy because You took all our burdens away. I guess You really just made the burdens more bearable. Still, that's something great to sing about, and it does bring happiness. I'm so glad You're there to lighten the load. As the world presses in and life feels heavy, remind me of the gift of song. It doesn't matter how good I sound or even what I sing, as long as it is praise to You. Thank You for carrying my burdens and lightening my load as I sing praise to You.*

## PRAISES

## PRAYER REQUESTS

## ANSWERS TO PRAYER

# Day 27
## ENJOY BEING ALIVE

*God, thank You for the passion You put inside of me. You inspire me with it.*
*When I am able to express that passion, I come alive in a special way. Thank You*
*for giving me a purpose. Please use my talents and passions to further Your kingdom*
*on earth. May I always have a heart for the things that stir my heart for You.*

### PRAYER REQUESTS

### PRAISES

### ANSWERS TO PRAYER

## Day 28
# SWEET ASSURANCE

My blessings are so many, my troubles are so few
How can I be discouraged when I know that I have You?
And I have the sweet assurance that there's nothing I need fear
If I but keep remembering I am Yours and You are near. . .
For anything and everything can somehow be endured
If Your presence is beside me and lovingly assured.

HELEN STEINER RICE

*Lord, my time with You is sweet. You have assured me that I have nothing to fear. I worry and spend time thinking what if. . .but it's really wasted time I could spend with You. Help me to focus on Your presence, Your closeness, and Your promise never to leave me.*

## PRAISES

## PRAYER REQUESTS

## ANSWERS TO PRAYER

## Day 29

# PRESENT REFLECTION

Reflect upon your present blessings, of which every man has many,
not on your past misfortunes, of which all men have some.

CHARLES DICKENS

*Father, the past is the past. I can't change it. I can only learn and grow from it. Thank You for forgiving and forgetting all my wrongs. I turn my eyes to today and set my course on the path before me. I will walk this path with You, assured of Your love and acceptance.*

## PRAYER REQUESTS

## PRAISES

## ANSWERS TO PRAYER

*Day 30*

# PROOF WE CAN RELY ON

At the end of each month I read over my prayer journal and see where God has done miraculous things. . . . If I can list a number of answers to specific prayers in January, I feel better prepared to trust God in February.

BILL HYBELS

*God, You do marvelous things each day. Thank You for the miracles in my life. When I am tempted to forget or feel sorry for myself, please bring the list of answered prayers before me. I never want to forget the depth of Your marvelous love for me.*

........................................................................................................

........................................................................................................

........................................................................................................

........................................................................................................

........................................................................................................

## PRAISES

........................................................

........................................................

........................................................

........................................................

........................................................

........................................................

........................................................

........................................................

## PRAYER REQUESTS

........................................................

........................................................

........................................................

## ANSWERS TO PRAYER

........................................................

........................................................

........................................................

*Day 31*

# GOD'S FAITHFULNESS

God has blessed us with a relationship with Himself. He is faithful to us too.
Despite our mistakes, God still loves us and gives us great blessings. . .
Let us believe God and walk faithfully in His way through all our days.

*God, You are forever faithful. Whatever You promise, You do. You cannot lie.
Knowing that makes it easier to trust you. Still, in my humanity, I struggle to
believe sometimes. Help me to believe, and may You find me faithful as well.*

## PRAYER REQUESTS

## PRAISES

## ANSWERS TO PRAYER

# WITH WORSHIP AND HONOR

Thanks be to you, Jesus Christ, for the many gifts Thou hast
bestowed on me. . . . I am giving Thee worship with my whole
life. . . . I am giving Thee honour with my whole utterance.

Carmina Gadelica

*Forgive me, Lord, when I go my own way. I don't mean to dishonor You with disobedience.
I get in a hurry and try to work things out on my own, which never ends well. Help me
to trust You and to follow You on the right path. Help me to listen to wisdom and obey.*

........................................................................................................................................................
........................................................................................................................................................
........................................................................................................................................................
........................................................................................................................................................
........................................................................................................................................................

## PRAISES

........................................................
........................................................
........................................................
........................................................
........................................................
........................................................
........................................................
........................................................
........................................................
........................................................

## PRAYER REQUESTS

........................................................
........................................................
........................................................
........................................................

## ANSWERS TO PRAYER

........................................................
........................................................
........................................................
........................................................

# Day 33
## INDULGE

Don't put off for tomorrow what you can do today,
because if you enjoy it today, you can do it again tomorrow.
JAMES A. MICHENER

*Lord, forgive me when I procrastinate. I don't want to sit in my excuses,
wishing I had done something. Help me to know when to wait on You and when
to take action. I want to be a person of action, ready and willing to do Your will.*

---

### PRAYER REQUESTS

### PRAISES

### ANSWERS TO PRAYER

*Day 34*
# REJOICE!

This is the day that the LORD has made; let us rejoice and be glad in it. . . .
Blessed is he who comes in the name of the LORD! We bless you from the house
of the LORD. The LORD is God, and he has made his light to shine upon us. . . .
You are my God, and I will give thanks to you; you are my God; I will extol you.

PSALM 118:24, 26–28 ESV

*Today counts. It's not an ordinary day but an extraordinary
day because You created this day for me. As I rejoice in You today,
show me how I can make this day special. Fill me with Your joy so that
I overflow with it onto other people. May they see You in my joy today.*

..................................................................................................................................

..................................................................................................................................

..................................................................................................................................

..................................................................................................................................

## PRAISES

..............................................................
..............................................................
..............................................................
..............................................................
..............................................................
..............................................................
..............................................................
..............................................................
..............................................................

## PRAYER REQUESTS

..............................................................
..............................................................
..............................................................
..............................................................

## ANSWERS TO PRAYER

..............................................................
..............................................................
..............................................................

# *Day 35*
# AWESOME GENEROSITY

What a wonderful, giving God we serve. He stands with extended hand, ready to give you the desires of your heart. Take a moment to offer thanks to Him for the greatest gifts, the awesome joys you've experienced, and even the small things that you realize He engineered to bless you in an unexpected way.

*Heavenly Father, I realize that You go above and beyond to give me good gifts. You always have Your hands open to me. You know what's in my heart. You know what I want before I ask, but You tell me to ask anyway. So today I ask for and receive all You have prepared for me.*

## PRAYER REQUESTS

## PRAISES

## ANSWERS TO PRAYER

# *Day 36*
## BLESS GOD

If you can eat today, enjoy the sunlight today, mix good
cheer with friends today, enjoy it and bless God for it.
HENRY WARD BEECHER

*Lord, thank You for friendship. I appreciate the people You have placed in my life.*
*Sometimes relationships are hard. But I want to be a blessing to others. Give me patience*
*and wisdom in the relationships I have. Show me how I can be a blessing to them.*

PRAISES

PRAYER REQUESTS

ANSWERS TO PRAYER

# Day 37
## ENJOYING GOOD HEALTH

*I thank You, Father, for giving me good health. There are so many who do not enjoy this blessing. Sometimes I'm tempted to complain about the aches and pains we all face from time to time, but I really have no reason to. You have been good to me. Give me wisdom in how to eat, exercise, and treat my body in a way that pleases You. You created my body, and You know every detail. Show me how to keep my immune system strong. Reveal to me what is good and acceptable in Your sight.*

### PRAYER REQUESTS

### PRAISES

### ANSWERS TO PRAYER

## Day 38

# A SPIRITUAL SCENT

God's holy beauty comes near you like a spiritual scent, and it stirs your drowsing soul. . . . He creates in you the desire to find Him and run after Him—to follow wherever He leads you, and to press peacefully against His heart wherever He is.

JOHN OF THE CROSS

*God, draw me near to You. Let my words of praise be a pleasing aroma to You. Stir my heart and show me who You are. I want to know You more. I will follow hard after You. May I never take my eyes off You, and may I stay in step with You all the days of my life.*

.......................................................................................................................................

.......................................................................................................................................

.......................................................................................................................................

.......................................................................................................................................

## PRAISES

## PRAYER REQUESTS

## ANSWERS TO PRAYER

## Day 39

# THE POWER OF LOVE

Love alone lightens every burden and makes the rough places
smooth. It bears every hardship as though it were nothing
and renders all bitterness sweet and acceptable.

THOMAS À KEMPIS

*Love is a powerful motivator. It caused You to give Your only Son as a ransom for my
soul. Thank You for making an incredible sacrifice so that I could be restored to You.
Now let my love for You motivate me to become all that You destined me to be.*

## PRAYER REQUESTS

## PRAISES

## ANSWERS TO PRAYER

# *Day 40*
# LET YOUR ADMIRATION SHOW

When I look at your heavens, the work of your fingers, the moon and the
stars, which you have set in place, what is man that you are mindful of him,
and the son of man that you care for him? Yet you have made him a little
lower than the heavenly beings and crowned him with glory and honor.

PSALM 8:3–5 ESV

*God of majesty and creative power, You formed the world with Your
words. You created this beautiful world and placed mankind in it so
that You could have fellowship with us. Thank You for creating me and
giving me life. May I live each day in a way that brings You glory.*

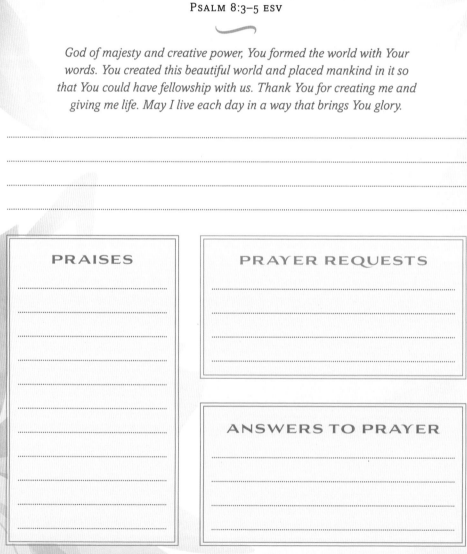

### PRAISES

### PRAYER REQUESTS

### ANSWERS TO PRAYER

## *Day 41*
# A GUIDEPOST FOR PRAYER

Our prayers should be for blessings in general,
for God knows best what is good for us.
SOCRATES

*Praise be to the God and Father of our Lord Jesus Christ. In Christ,
God has given us every spiritual blessing in the heavenly world. That is,
in Christ, he chose us before the world was made so that we would be his
holy people—people without blame before him (Ephesians 1:3–4 NCV).*

......................................................................................................................................
......................................................................................................................................
......................................................................................................................................
......................................................................................................................................
......................................................................................................................................

## PRAYER REQUESTS

......................................................................
......................................................................
......................................................................
......................................................................

## PRAISES

......................................................................
......................................................................
......................................................................
......................................................................
......................................................................
......................................................................
......................................................................
......................................................................
......................................................................

## ANSWERS TO PRAYER

......................................................................
......................................................................
......................................................................
......................................................................

*Day 42*

# FOR LITTLE THINGS

Thank you, God, for little things that often come our way,
The things we take for granted but don't mention when we pray.
The unexpected courtesy, the thoughtful kindly deed,
A hand reached out to help us in the time of sudden need.

<small>HELEN STEINER RICE</small>

*God, thank You for the blessings, big and small. In no matter what order
I count them, You provided them all. Please allow me to be a blessing
to someone as I go about my day. I open my heart willingly to hear You
as You lead. I never want to miss an opportunity to sow a seed.*

## PRAISES

## PRAYER REQUESTS

## ANSWERS TO PRAYER

# Day 43

## RESTORED LIVING

We all know what it feels like to be at rest. . . . But are we willing to
leave the press long enough to lie down in the soothing green pastures
and to be led by the still waters of His provision? That, my friend,
is not resort living but restored living. And each of us needs it.

PATSY CLAIRMONT

*Today I refuse to believe the lie that I always need to be busy. Thank You for the
example in Genesis where You rested. I will intentionally take time to rest my body
and my mind. Please use those times to speak to me as I meditate on Your goodness.*

### PRAYER REQUESTS

### PRAISES

### ANSWERS TO PRAYER

# BLESSED FRIENDS

Nothing opens the heart like another person with whom
you may share all your hopes, fears, and joys.
UNKNOWN

~~~

*God, You know I hold my dreams tightly. I don't share them with just anyone. So thank
You for sending me those people who love me unconditionally. I appreciate that they
don't judge me or my dreams. Help me to be supportive of their dreams as well.*

........................................................................................................................................

........................................................................................................................................

........................................................................................................................................

........................................................................................................................................

........................................................................................................................................

........................................................................................................................................

## PRAISES

..............................................

..............................................

..............................................

..............................................

..............................................

..............................................

..............................................

..............................................

..............................................

..............................................

## PRAYER REQUESTS

..............................................

..............................................

..............................................

..............................................

..............................................

## ANSWERS TO PRAYER

..............................................

..............................................

..............................................

# Day 45
## OPEN UP!

He is always willing to relieve our needs. The chief thing lacking is a suitable disposition on our part to receive His grace and blessing.

JOHN WESLEY

*God, pride causes me to miss out on things sometimes. I don't want to be so prideful, unwilling to accept gifts or help, that I miss You along the way. I open up my heart to others today. I receive Your grace and blessing, even when it comes from someone else's hands.*

### PRAYER REQUESTS

### PRAISES

### ANSWERS TO PRAYER

# Day 46

## WHOLLY HIS

How blessed is God! And what a blessing he is! He's the Father of our
Master, Jesus Christ, and takes us to the high places of blessing in him. Long
before he laid down earth's foundations, he had us in mind, had settled
on us as the focus of his love, to be made whole and holy by his love.

EPHESIANS 1:3–4 MSG

*No one compares to You, God. You are Creator and the Father of Jesus,
my Redeemer. Before the foundations of the world, I was on Your mind.
It's hard for me to even imagine, and yet Your love saved me and
made me in Your image. I am so blessed and thankful for You.*

### PRAISES

### PRAYER REQUESTS

### ANSWERS TO PRAYER

# MAKING A CONNECTION

The joy of receiving is far more than the gifts—that when we receive graciously
and gladly, we reciprocate the gift with joy and gratitude; and in that moment
of shared happiness and understanding, giver and receiver "connect."
JENNY WALTON

*I am beyond elated when I find myself in Your presence, Lord. Sometimes You
make Yourself known quietly. Other times You surprise me with a grand entrance of
something wonderful You orchestrated just for me. I am honored to belong to You.*

## PRAYER REQUESTS

## PRAISES

## ANSWERS TO PRAYER

*Day 48*

# THE ART OF LIFE

The art of life is to live in the present moment and to make
that moment as perfect as we can by the realization that we
are the instruments and expression of God Himself.

EMMET FOX

*You created me for today. It's not Your plan for me to look back in sorrow or regret or to
look forward in dread or even anticipation, wishing I were already there. Today is the
day. I will enjoy the experience You've set before me and live in the moment called today.*

## PRAISES

## PRAYER REQUESTS

## ANSWERS TO PRAYER

# Day 49
## PEACEMAKERS, REJOICE!

God blesses our efforts for peace, though they may not bear fruit immediately. We draw closer to God, even if we cannot improve the lives of others. God doesn't command that we will be successful in our peacemaking, though we may be. He only requires us to work at it. Blessings for that obedience will still come from His hand.

*I am a peacemaker. It doesn't honor You when I dredge up drama or stir up chaos. Relationships are sticky because of our humanity. Help me to find my joy by following Your peace. I will seek peace and let it serve as the referee in my life.*

......................................................................................................................................
......................................................................................................................................
......................................................................................................................................
......................................................................................................................................
......................................................................................................................................

### PRAYER REQUESTS
......................................................................
......................................................................
......................................................................
......................................................................

### ANSWERS TO PRAYER
......................................................................
......................................................................
......................................................................
......................................................................

### PRAISES
......................................................................
......................................................................
......................................................................
......................................................................
......................................................................
......................................................................
......................................................................
......................................................................
......................................................................

*Day 50*

# BLESSED SOLITUDE

I feel the same way about solitude as some people feel about the blessing of
the church. It's the light of grace for me. I never close my door behind me
without the awareness that I am carrying out an act of mercy toward myself.
PETER HOEG

*Today I get away with You, my God! I want to enjoy the solitude.
I rest my mind on You. I enjoy the quiet moments doing simple things
or simply nothing at all. Pour out Your peace in these few minutes that
only You and I share. Remind me to quiet my soul and rest in You.*

## PRAISES

## PRAYER REQUESTS

## ANSWERS TO PRAYER

# *Day 51*
# FULL-CIRCLE BLESSINGS

If you affirm goodness, goodness will be there; if you affirm love,
love will be there; if you affirm thankfulness, blessings will come.
A good place to begin is by giving praise and thanks to Almighty God.
NORMAN VINCENT PEALE

*Today I celebrate Your goodness that is at work in my life. I affirm Your love that is*
*always there for me. I am thankful for Your presence and Your peace. I praise You*
*for the blessings You graciously bestow upon my life. Thank You for being my God.*

## PRAYER REQUESTS

## PRAISES

## ANSWERS TO PRAYER

*Day 52*

# STOP CHASING

I say it is better to be content with what little you have. Otherwise,
you will always be struggling for more, and that is like chasing the wind.

ECCLESIASTES 4:6 NCV

*Lord, I push too hard sometimes. Hard work and perseverance are good qualities,
but it's good to also be content. Help me to set in-between goals and enjoy the little
moments of achievement too. I am thankful for what I have. It is enough for today.*

## PRAISES

## PRAYER REQUESTS

## ANSWERS TO PRAYER

# Day 53

## GENERATIONS OF THANKS

God help us to be grateful for our blessings, never to be guilty of the sin of ingratitude, and to instill this same gratitude into the lives of our children.

EZRA TAFT BENSON

*Forgive me, Lord, when I've been ungrateful or thought I deserved more. Even if I didn't get what I thought I deserved, You set the path before me. You provide what I need. Help me to always have a heart of gratitude, and check my attitude when needed.*

## PRAYER REQUESTS

## PRAISES

## ANSWERS TO PRAYER

# *Day 54*
# WAYSIDE SACRAMENTS

Never lose an opportunity of seeing anything beautiful. Beauty is
God's handwriting—a wayside sacrament; welcome it in every fair face,
every fair sky, every fair flower, and thank for it Him. . .[as] a cup of blessing.

CHARLES KINGSLEY

*Lord, this life is ugly sometimes because it is a fallen world. But because You
created it, I can see beauty and celebrate it. Please point out the beauty for me.
Help me to have a filter on my perspective to see Your beauty in the darkness.*

## PRAISES

## PRAYER REQUESTS

## ANSWERS TO PRAYER

## Day 55
# NO MORE DISTRACTIONS

When we put aside the things that would distract us from God, our lives are fully blessed. We can worship Him for the things He has given us—the physical and spiritual joys that leap off our tongues as we think of all our Savior has given.

*Forgive me! I have been so distracted. I have had my head down, trying to figure things out on my own. Today I look up and focus where I should. Thank You for getting my attention. I will keep my eyes on You.*

## PRAYER REQUESTS

## PRAISES

## ANSWERS TO PRAYER

# DISCOVER LIFE'S BLESSINGS

As we grow in our capacities to discover the joys that God has placed in our lives, life becomes a glorious experience of discovering His endless wonders.

*I remember the joy that flooded my soul when I first came to know You. Your wonders filled me everywhere I looked. Bring back that newness again. Flood my soul with the joy that can come only from You. Let me see Your endless wonders like I did back then.*

## PRAISES

## PRAYER REQUESTS

## ANSWERS TO PRAYER

## Day 57
# PRICELESS GIFTS

This brings you a million good wishes and more.
For the things you cannot buy in a store—
Like faith to sustain you in times of trial,
A joy-filled heart and a happy smile,
Contentment, inner peace, and love—
All priceless gifts from God above!
HELEN STEINER RICE

*Thank You, Father, for the gift of faith. You give me the strength to stand firm, believing You will bring me through, no matter what I face. Though I stumble over the things I don't understand, You hold me up. Wherever I go, You see me through to the other side.*

## PRAYER REQUESTS

## PRAISES

## ANSWERS TO PRAYER

# GENEROUS HEARTS

The world of the generous gets larger and larger. . . . The one who blesses
others is abundantly blessed; those who help others are helped.

PROVERBS 11:24–25 MSG

*Lord, give me a compassion like Yours to love others. Give me the means to bless others in
their time of need. When I open my mouth, I will encourage and speak life to those who
need it. I will walk with an open hand, willing to give to those You bring into my life.*

## PRAISES

## PRAYER REQUESTS

## ANSWERS TO PRAYER

# Day 59
## REKINDLED AWARENESS

In everyone's life, at some time, our inner fire goes out. It is then burst
into flame by an encounter with another human being. We should
all be thankful for those people who rekindle the inner spirit.

ALBERT SCHWEITZER

*Lord, thank You for putting people in my life who spark the flame of hope. You've made
sure someone said what I needed to hear from You in my darkest hour. Let me be that
igniting flame in the life of someone else. Fill my mouth with the words they need to hear.*

## PRAYER REQUESTS

## PRAISES

## ANSWERS TO PRAYER

*Day 60*

# GLORIOUS DAY

It is the first mild day of March: each minute sweeter than before. . . .
There is a blessing in the air, which seems a sense of joy to yield.

WILLIAM WORDSWORTH

*Today I celebrate the life You've given to me! Thank You for the beauty around me and the purpose You've given me to praise You all of my days. Your joy doesn't depend on my circumstances. I will embrace the joy You've given me. I receive it by faith each morning.*

## PRAISES

## PRAYER REQUESTS

## ANSWERS TO PRAYER

# Day 61
## SATISFIED!

Continue to walk steadily with your Lord, and He'll fulfill many more desires. Then, at the end of life, you'll see that any He left behind were best done so, and you'll offer this one-word testimony: satisfied!

*God in heaven, You satisfy my soul. You fill my heart with good things. As long as You give me breath, I know I have work to do. Thank You for the dreams you've placed within me. I am satisfied to walk in the moment with You.*

PRAYER REQUESTS

PRAISES

ANSWERS TO PRAYER

# Day 62
## ETERNAL NOURISHMENT

*Give us, O Father, all things needful for our souls and bodies, not only the meat that perishes, but the sacramental bread, and Your grace, the food that endures to everlasting life. You feed my soul with good things. Your Word is filled with spiritual protein and desserts. I am satisfied every day as I fill up with Your truth. Give me a deeper hunger to know You. Thank You for keeping me healthy in spirit, mind, and body.*

### PRAISES

### PRAYER REQUESTS

### ANSWERS TO PRAYER

## Day 63

# THE NEVER-ENDING RESOURCE

*Prayer is. . .a mine which is never exhausted. . . . It is the root,
the fountain, the mother of a thousand blessings.*
JOHN CHRYSOSTOM

*I open my mouth in prayer, and You meet me wherever I am. You are
always there for me. I put You first in all things. Help me to always go to
You in prayer for every decision. I seek Your counsel. Forgive me when I
look to mankind for answers. The best and final answers are in You.*

.......................................................................................................................
.......................................................................................................................
.......................................................................................................................
.......................................................................................................................
.......................................................................................................................

### PRAYER REQUESTS

.............................................................
.............................................................
.............................................................
.............................................................

### PRAISES

.............................................................
.............................................................
.............................................................
.............................................................
.............................................................
.............................................................
.............................................................
.............................................................
.............................................................
.............................................................
.............................................................

### ANSWERS TO PRAYER

.............................................................
.............................................................
.............................................................
.............................................................

# Day 64
## STEADY BLESSINGS

"If you follow my decrees and are careful to obey my commands, I will send you rain in its season, and the ground will yield its crops and the trees their fruit. Your threshing will continue until grape harvest and the grape harvest will continue until planting, and you will eat all the food you want and live in safety in your land."

LEVITICUS 26:3–5 NIV

*I want to be found faithful to Your commands, Lord. I surrender my heart to You. I give You all of me. I will be careful to obey Your commands not just because of the promised blessing in obedience but also because I love You. Thank You for Your faithfulness.*

### PRAISES

### PRAYER REQUESTS

### ANSWERS TO PRAYER

# Day 65

## ALL THAT IS

All that is good, all that is true, all that is beautiful, all that is beneficent,
be it great or small, be it perfect or fragmentary, natural as well as
supernatural, moral as well as material, comes from God.

JOHN NEWMAN

*It is only in Your goodness that I want to live. I give thanks to You today for every blessing You give to me. You are good. And all things work together for my good. Thank You for taking the broken pieces of my life and repairing me. I am made new in You.*

### PRAYER REQUESTS

### PRAISES

### ANSWERS TO PRAYER

# Day 66
## MEMORIES

Memories are the treasures that we keep locked deep within the
storehouse of our souls, to keep our hearts warm when we are lonely.
BECKY ALIGADA

*Thank You, Lord, for all my memories. The painful ones make me realize You are
my Savior and healer. The good ones bring me back to just how miraculous my life
really is because I choose You. Help me to never forget why I live each day for You.*

........................................................................................................
........................................................................................................
........................................................................................................
........................................................................................................
........................................................................................................
........................................................................................................

### PRAISES

### PRAYER REQUESTS

### ANSWERS TO PRAYER

# *Day 67*
## TRUE COLORS

God offers us His Spirit not just as an encouragement but as a heart changer. He enters into us and begins to redesign our interior life. Suddenly, our actions and our words are truthful, kind, and fair. No longer do they reflect the blackness that painted our hearts; they are now shining with the rainbow colors of His blessings.

*Before You, God, my life was empty and gray. Your joy changed me from the inside out. You filled my life with every color and hue. Your Spirit redesigns my life, constantly bringing new revelations to me so that I may understand Your purpose and follow You all my days.*

...............................................................................................................................................

...............................................................................................................................................

...............................................................................................................................................

...............................................................................................................................................

...............................................................................................................................................

### PRAYER REQUESTS

### PRAISES

### ANSWERS TO PRAYER

## *Day 68*
# HUNGER FOR BLESSINGS

It seems to me we can never give up longing and wishing while
we are thoroughly alive. There are certain things we feel to be
beautiful and good, and we must hunger after them.

GEORGE ELIOT

*Moses asked to see Your face, and You hid him in the cleft of the rock as You passed
by. I long to experience You, God, in a tangible way. Your presence is everything to me.
Thank You for Your goodness that satisfies my soul. May I forever hunger for You.*

............................................................................................................................................................
............................................................................................................................................................
............................................................................................................................................................
............................................................................................................................................................

| PRAISES | PRAYER REQUESTS |
|---|---|
| | |
| | **ANSWERS TO PRAYER** |

# Day 69
## TRUE BLISS

The real joy of life is in its play. Play is anything we do for the joy and love of doing it, apart from any profit, compulsion, or sense of duty. It is the real living of life.

WALTER RAUSCHENBUSCH

*Thank You for the passion You've placed in my soul. I appreciate the opportunity to do those things I truly enjoy. I am grateful to have things in my life that bring me joy. When I'm doing those things that bring You joy, I feel alive.*

## PRAYER REQUESTS

## PRAISES

## ANSWERS TO PRAYER

# Day 70
## NO WORRIES

"Therefore I say to you, do not worry about your life, what you will eat; nor about the body, what you will put on. Life is more than food, and the body is more than clothing. Consider the ravens, for they neither sow nor reap, which have neither storehouse nor barn; and God feeds them. Of how much more value are you than the birds?"

LUKE 12:22–24 NKJV

*I have a need to feel secure, and I admit that having money in the bank and food in the freezer can give me a false sense of security. Help me, Lord, to let go of those things and trust You to provide everything I need. You will take care of me. You always have!*

PRAISES

PRAYER REQUESTS

ANSWERS TO PRAYER

# Day 71
## GO WITH GOD

May the road rise to meet you, May the wind be always at your back,
May the sun shine warm upon your face, May the rain fall soft upon your fields,
And, until we meet again, May God hold you in the palm of His hand.

IRISH BLESSING

*The life You give me, God, is good. Your blessings are new every morning. You hold me in the palm of Your hand. I am always on Your mind. You will never forget about me or leave me alone. I choose to go anywhere as long as I am with You.*

### PRAYER REQUESTS

### PRAISES

### ANSWERS TO PRAYER

## *Day 72*
# BE GLAD

Be glad of life, because it gives you the chance to love and to work and to play
and to look up at the stars; to be satisfied with your possessions. . .to think
seldom of your enemies, often of your friends, and every day of Christ.

HENRY VAN DYKE

*Each day is a gift from You, Lord. I give You thanks for each chance to love, work,
and play in this beautiful creation You made for me. I never want to take Your
gifts for granted. Most of all, I am thankful to have a relationship with You.*

## PRAISES

## PRAYER REQUESTS

## ANSWERS TO PRAYER

# NEVER APART

Would God give a sparrow all it needs for life and leave a human out of the loop? Obviously, the Creator doesn't forget or ignore anything. Without Him, earth wouldn't exist. The universe can't keep its course apart from His command. But sometimes we wonder if we've somehow disconnected from God. All along, God never forgets our needs.

*God, I am always on Your mind. You hold me in the palm of Your hand. You keep me in all of my ways. Even when it feels like I'm alone, disconnected from You, help me remember that You will always remember me. You know what I need before I even ask.*

## PRAYER REQUESTS

## PRAISES

## ANSWERS TO PRAYER

# COUNT THE GOOD THINGS

When we start to count flowers, we cease to count weeds;
When we start to count blessings, we cease to count needs;
When we start to count laughter, we cease to count tears;
When we count happy memories, we cease to count years.

UNKNOWN

*Heavenly Father, help me to always remember to look at the things in my life from a positive perspective. You've given me everything good in my life. Help me to find the simplest of joys in every aspect of my life and share that with others.*

## PRAISES

## PRAYER REQUESTS

## ANSWERS TO PRAYER

# BLESS OTHERS

The Bible most often refers to human abilities as gifts because they are given in order to be given again. . . . God expects you to strengthen and polish [your gifts] and use [them] to enrich the lives of others. . . . As you use your gifts to bless others, you will be blessed most of all.

*God, sometimes I don't even recognize the gifts You've given me to share. Help me to see what You've placed within me to benefit others. As I give by faith to others and respond to You as You lead me, give me confidence and strength to do what You ask of me.*

## PRAYER REQUESTS

## PRAISES

## ANSWERS TO PRAYER

## Day 76
# BOUNTIFUL BLESSINGS

And God is able to bless you abundantly, so that in all things at
all times, having all that you need, you will abound in every
good work. As it is written: "They have freely scattered their
gifts to the poor; their righteousness endures forever."

2 CORINTHIANS 9:8–9 NIV

*Gracious God, thank You for providing everything I need. Give me Your wisdom to
discern needs from wants. Open my eyes to see You at work in my circumstances so that
I am able to rise above any disappointment, trusting Your timing is always perfect.*

## PRAISES

## PRAYER REQUESTS

## ANSWERS TO PRAYER

## Day 77
# HIS DELIGHTFUL TOUCH

The Lord gives you the experience of enjoying His presence. He touches you,
and His touch is so delightful that, more than ever, you are drawn inwardly to Him.

JEANNE GUYON

*Father, draw me closer to You today. May I feel Your presence in a tangible way. Let
me notice the small things You do in my life and be ever grateful. I am delighted in
You. I belong to You. Thank You for touching me and calling me Your own child.*

........................................................................................................

........................................................................................................

........................................................................................................

........................................................................................................

........................................................................................................

........................................................................................................

## PRAYER REQUESTS

........................................................

........................................................

........................................................

........................................................

## PRAISES

........................................................

........................................................

........................................................

........................................................

........................................................

........................................................

........................................................

........................................................

........................................................

## ANSWERS TO PRAYER

........................................................

........................................................

........................................................

........................................................

## Day 78
# MORE THAN WE SEEK

Each day there are showers of blessings sent from the Father above,
For God is a great, lavish giver, and there is no end to His love. . .
For no matter how big man's dreams are, God's blessings are infinitely more,
For always God's giving is greater than what man is asking for.
HELEN STEINER RICE

*God, You are infinitely more than I could ever imagine. Your good gifts are lavish in my life. Thank You for the dreams You've placed in my life. Give me hope to see them through. On my own, I can't, but I trust You to see all my dreams come true.*

### PRAISES

### PRAYER REQUESTS

### ANSWERS TO PRAYER

# Day 79

## SLOW DOWN!

Don't let yourself get so busy that you miss those little but important extras in life—the beauty of a day. . .the smile of a friend. . .the serenity of a quiet moment alone. For it is often life's smallest pleasures and gentlest joys that make the biggest and most lasting difference.

*Today I will take time to sit with You, Lord. You have given me the smallest things in life to bring great joy. I receive Your blessings. I drink those moments in, filling up my soul. Help me to pause and reflect and not be so busy that I miss the little things in life.*

PRAYER REQUESTS

PRAISES

ANSWERS TO PRAYER

# A PERFECT CIRCLE

A circle has no beginning and no ending. The circle of blessing can
begin at any point within it. The circle is made up of quiet actions,
love, simple gratitude, forgiveness, generous gifts, trust, precious
memories, a heart that knows what to remember and what to forget.

UNKNOWN

*Thank You, God, for being the Alpha and Omega, the beginning and the end. You know
me like no one else does. Thank You for Your quiet love. May I always respond to You
with simple gratitude and trust. May I forgive others as quickly as You've forgiven me.*

.................................................................................................................................................

.................................................................................................................................................

.................................................................................................................................................

.................................................................................................................................................

.................................................................................................................................................

## PRAISES

## PRAYER REQUESTS

## ANSWERS TO PRAYER

# *Day 81*
## NOW AND ALWAYS

Father, thank You for all You have given me, for all You have
taught me, and for all the good times still to come. Amen.

*Help me to live my life focused on eternity and to perceive it not as far off but
as a part of today. You are with me now and always. I rely on You. You hold
me in the palm of Your hand. You have all the answers I will ever need.*

........................................................................................................................
........................................................................................................................
........................................................................................................................
........................................................................................................................
........................................................................................................................
........................................................................................................................
........................................................................................................................

### PRAYER REQUESTS

........................................................
........................................................
........................................................
........................................................

### PRAISES

........................................................
........................................................
........................................................
........................................................
........................................................
........................................................
........................................................
........................................................
........................................................
........................................................
........................................................
........................................................
........................................................

### ANSWERS TO PRAYER

........................................................
........................................................
........................................................

# Day 82

## HELP IS NEAR

Yet the LORD longs to be gracious to you; therefore he will rise up to show you compassion. For the LORD is a God of justice. Blessed are all who wait for him!
ISAIAH 30:18 NIV

*Lord, waiting is hard. I know You understand that because You walked on the earth as a man. Thank You for the examples You gave to show me the heart of the Father. I am grateful for His grace, compassion, and justice. Help me to see the blessings in waiting.*

### PRAISES

### PRAYER REQUESTS

### ANSWERS TO PRAYER

# BRIGHT MOMENTS

Trust that any unclear moments will bring you to that moment of
clarity and action when you are known by God and know Him.
These are better and brighter moments of His blessing.

~

*God, I want to know You; I want to see You. I want to understand You in a deeper
way. Thank You for your unconditional love. Teach me to hear Your voice and
to recognize You at work in my life. Bring me to a place of quiet rest in You.*

PRAYER REQUESTS

PRAISES

ANSWERS TO PRAYER

*Day 84*

# RELISH THE GOOD. . .AND BAD

The marvelous richness of human experience would lose something of rewarding joy if there were no limitations to overcome. The hilltop hour would not be half so wonderful if there were no dark valleys to traverse.

HELEN KELLER

*Yes, faith is the substance of things hoped for and the evidence of what I've not yet seen. Each day requires me to stretch beyond the natural things in life and experience the things You have set in motion that I cannot yet grasp.*

......................................................................................................................

......................................................................................................................

......................................................................................................................

......................................................................................................................

| PRAISES | PRAYER REQUESTS |
|---|---|
| | |
| | ANSWERS TO PRAYER |
| | |

## Day 85

# THE GREATEST PROMISE

A rainbow stretches from one end of the sky to the other. Each shade of color, each facet of light, displays the radiant spectrum of God's love—a promise that He will always love each one of us at our worst and at our best.

*God, it's when I am at my worst that I feel like I need You most. I am grateful for Your grace that covers me when I fall and Your matchless love that reaches down and brings me back up. Your forgiveness sets me on a path to everything good.*

PRAYER REQUESTS

PRAISES

ANSWERS TO PRAYER

## Day 86

# INCOMPARABLE LOVE

All the joy and delight, all the pleasures a thousand worlds could offer, are as dust in the balance when weighed against one hour of this mutual exchange of love and communion with the Lord.

CORA HARRIS MACILRAVY

*If I could travel the worlds You created, nothing I ever encounter could compare to the time I am able to spend in Your presence. Thank You for the gift of time with You. May I always cherish it and prefer it to anything else going on in my life.*

---

## PRAISES

## PRAYER REQUESTS

## ANSWERS TO PRAYER

# BEYOND OUR ASKING

More than hearts can imagine or minds comprehend,
God's bountiful gifts are ours without end.
We ask for a cupful when the vast sea is ours.
We pick a small rosebud from a garden of flowers. . . .
Whatever we ask for falls short of God's giving,
For His greatness exceeds every facet of living.

HELEN STEINER RICE

*Father, the gifts You offer me are far beyond what I can comprehend. Help me
to dream bigger and to believe I can do all things because of Christ in me.
I want to leave this world having fulfilled the destiny You placed within me.*

## PRAYER REQUESTS

## PRAISES

## ANSWERS TO PRAYER

# ASK, KNOCK, SEEK

"I say to you, ask, and what you ask for will be given to you. Look,
and what you are looking for you will find. Knock, and the door you are
knocking on will be opened to you. For everyone who asks, will receive
what he asks for. Everyone who looks, will find what he is looking
for. Everyone who knocks, will have the door opened to him."

LUKE 11:9–10 NLV

*Lord, sometimes it's hard for me to ask because I don't really know what I need.
Teach me to ask for Your will, Your purpose, and Your plan. Today I ask for Your will.
I knock on the door You set before me, and I receive whatever You have for me by faith.*

## PRAISES

## PRAYER REQUESTS

## ANSWERS TO PRAYER

# Day 89

## SWEET HOUR OF PRAYER

Sweet hour of prayer! Sweet hour of prayer! The joys I feel, the bliss I share,
Of those whose anxious spirits burn with strong desires for thy return!
With such I hasten to the place where God my Savior shows His face,
And gladly take my station there, and wait for thee, sweet hour of prayer!

WILLIAM WALFORD

*Savior, prayer is simple. I know I can talk to You from my heart. But the distractions pull me into a busyness, and I don't always make time for You. Forgive me and help me to cherish the quiet moments in prayer. I choose to make time with You a priority today.*

### PRAYER REQUESTS

### PRAISES

### ANSWERS TO PRAYER

# Day 90
## PATIENT FAITH

*Dear Lord, thank You for my life and everything in it: the good, the bad, and all the future blessings that I know You'll send my way. Help me to recognize the trials in my life as Your gifts in disguise and to wait patiently as Your plan comes to fruition in my life. You make everything good in Your time. I know the hardships and difficulties are just for a season. Help me to see that no matter how hard things can be, You will use it to bring blessing to my life. I will trust You and hold on to You. I pray You find me always faithful.*

### PRAISES

### PRAYER REQUESTS

### ANSWERS TO PRAYER

# Day 91

## A STEADY STREAM

Even in the midst of our worst troubles, we can trust that, as Jesus said,
God still remembers how to give good gifts. Though we may not like
our situation, God's ability to give good things hasn't dried up.

*Sometimes it feels like a steady stream of unfortunate things occur. When those
bad things happen, remind me that You are a good father, looking to give
good gifts to me, Your child. Open my eyes to see the good in all things.*

## PRAYER REQUESTS

## PRAISES

## ANSWERS TO PRAYER

*Day 92*

# OUR FATHER'S WORLD

Everywhere across the land you see God's face and touch His hand
Each time you look up in the sky or watch the fluffy clouds drift by,
Or hear a bluebird brightly sing, or see the winter turn to spring,
Or touch a leaf or see a tree, it's all God whispering, "This is Me. . ."
HELEN STEINER RICE

*When I look at all You have created, the wonder of this world, I see proof
of Your existence and better understand who You are. Each glimpse I
take of Your beauty reminds me that You did everything so that You
could have a family, so that You could have fellowship with me.*

## PRAISES

## PRAYER REQUESTS

## ANSWERS TO PRAYER

# Day 93

## BLESSED SHOWERS

The enormous wealth of love God has for you compels Him to shower you with His presence and draw you close to Him. The fresh scent that remains after a spring rain shower is an open invitation to rest in His mercy and grace. . .His gentle desire to satisfy your heart with everything good.

*The pitter-patter of the rain brings an unexplainable calm. It ushers me into Your presence and causes me to reflect on who You are. You are everything good. Thank You for Your generous mercy and grace at work in my life.*

.......................................................................................................................
.......................................................................................................................
.......................................................................................................................
.......................................................................................................................
.......................................................................................................................

### PRAYER REQUESTS

.........................................................
.........................................................
.........................................................
.........................................................

### ANSWERS TO PRAYER

.........................................................
.........................................................
.........................................................
.........................................................

### PRAISES

.........................................................
.........................................................
.........................................................
.........................................................
.........................................................
.........................................................
.........................................................
.........................................................
.........................................................
.........................................................
.........................................................

# ALLOVER BLESSINGS

I said to myself, "Relax and rest. GOD has showered you with
blessings. Soul, you've been rescued from death; Eye, you've been
rescued from tears; and you, Foot, were kept from stumbling."
PSALM 116:7–8 MSG

*God, I pause today and catch my breath. I don't have to run in fear anymore
but can rest in You, knowing You have saved me. You have given me life
everlasting. I can stop looking over my shoulder and just look to You.*

## PRAISES

## PRAYER REQUESTS

## ANSWERS TO PRAYER

## Day 95
# THINGS TO COME

If God hath made this world so fair, where sin and death abound,
How beautiful beyond compare. Will paradise be found!
JAMES MONTGOMERY

*Thank You, Jesus, for going to heaven to prepare a place for me. I can't fathom the wonder of that place where I will spend forever with You. This earth is filled with extraordinary things, but how much more will that eternal city be.*

PRAYER REQUESTS

PRAISES

ANSWERS TO PRAYER

*Day 96*

# WORLDLY RICHES VS. GOD'S RICHES

Nothing more clearly shows how little God esteems his gift to men of wealth, money, position, and other worldly goods, than the way he distributes these, and the sort of men who are most amply provided with them.

JEAN DE LA BRUYÈRE

*Lord, what a vast difference between what is important to You and what most people on earth value. Help me to highly esteem the souls over any material thing. For souls are truly the currency of heaven. May I keep that truth before me all my days.*

## PRAISES

## PRAYER REQUESTS

## ANSWERS TO PRAYER

*Day 97*

# UNCONDITIONAL LOVE

A simple pleasure like the unconditional love of a dog reminds us that though we may stray, God always calls us back to the home of His heart.

*God, life demands my attention to so many things. I can become distracted. May I never miss an opportunity You have for me. I set my heart on You. Give me ears to hear Your voice as Your love calls me to always return to You.*

## PRAYER REQUESTS

## PRAISES

## ANSWERS TO PRAYER

# Day 98
## TAKE NOTHING FOR GRANTED

It is generally true that all that is required to make men unmindful of what they owe God for any blessing is that they should receive that blessing often and regularly.

RICHARD WHATELY

*God, help me to remember that all I am and all I have is because You gave it to me. Provide me with a way of escape from ungratefulness and entitlement. I came into this world with nothing. All I am I owe to You. Thank You for each blessing big or small.*

## PRAISES

## PRAYER REQUESTS

## ANSWERS TO PRAYER

## Day 99

# JOY AND RIGHTEOUSNESS

Our Lord has purchased joy as well as righteousness for us. It is the very design of the gospel that, being saved from guilt, we should be happy in the love of Christ.

JOHN WESLEY

*In Christ alone I have joy. I am free from shame or guilt because of the exchange He made—giving His life for mine. I can stand before the throne of grace without sin. Thank You, Father, for accepting me as Your own. My joy is always in You.*

### PRAYER REQUESTS

### ANSWERS TO PRAYER

### PRAISES

# Day 100

## THE SOURCE OF WEALTH

You may say to yourself, "My power and the strength of my hands
have produced this wealth for me." But remember the LORD your
God, for it is he who gives you the ability to produce wealth.
DEUTERONOMY 8:17–18 NIV

*Lord, thank You for giving me the ability to produce wealth. You make a way each day
for everything I put my hand on to become prosperous. You have blessed me to be a
blessing. Let Your provision in my life be a testimony of Your goodness and Your love.*

### PRAISES

### PRAYER REQUESTS

### ANSWERS TO PRAYER

*Day 101*

# GOD CARES

*Father, Your correction lasts only a moment, but its blessings are eternal. When I realize You are so concerned for me and want to help me, I am filled with gratitude and am willing to be led in the right direction. When You speak, I will listen. I hear Your voice, and a stranger's voice I will not follow. Help me to obey quickly and turn in the direction You would have me go. My thanksgiving for Your presence in my life overflows. All my days I choose to follow You.*

## PRAYER REQUESTS

## ANSWERS TO PRAYER

## PRAISES

# Day 102
## HOME

What is home? A roof to keep out rain? Four walls to keep out the wind?
Floors to keep out the cold? Yes, but home is more than that. It is the
laugh of a baby, the warmth of loving hearts, lights from happy eyes,
kindness, loyalty, comradeship. . . . That is home. God bless it!
UNKNOWN

*God, thank You for blessing my home. It's not the physical building that I live in but the
relationships shared with those who go in and out its door. Thank You for each person
who feels like home to me. May You minister to them and keep them in all their ways.*

PRAISES

PRAYER REQUESTS

ANSWERS TO PRAYER

# Day 103
## GOD'S INTENTION

When we thank God for His blessings and use them properly—to help others and support our families in a responsible Christian lifestyle—worldly goods become blessings He can use through us. That's just what God intended.

*God, I want to be the blessing You intended me to be. When You speak to my heart to share the blessings in my life with others, I will obey quickly. I will give with a cheerful heart to others. Help me to live my life with hands open, willing to give and receive.*

........................................................................................
........................................................................................
........................................................................................
........................................................................................
........................................................................................
........................................................................................

### PRAYER REQUESTS

........................................................
........................................................
........................................................
........................................................

### PRAISES

........................................................
........................................................
........................................................
........................................................
........................................................
........................................................
........................................................
........................................................
........................................................
........................................................

### ANSWERS TO PRAYER

........................................................
........................................................
........................................................
........................................................

# GOD'S BOUQUET

All the flowers God has made are beautiful. The rose in its
glory and the lily in its whiteness do not rob the tiny violet of
its sweet smell, or the daisy of its charming simplicity.

THÉRÈSE OF LISIEUX

*God, the world tries to divide us through our differences, but You made us
uniquely individual on purpose. Help me to remember to celebrate the differences
in others. Show me how we fit together to honor You and bring You glory.*

## PRAISES

## PRAYER REQUESTS

## ANSWERS TO PRAYER

# Day 105

# BUTTERFLIES

Happiness is as a butterfly, which, when pursued, is always beyond
your grasp, but which, if you will sit down quietly, may alight upon you.

Nathaniel Hawthorne

*Lord, help me to remember that happiness is not something I need to chase after.
Instead, as I live my life looking to You, the author and finisher of my faith, You
bring the greatest joys to my life, especially when I least expect it. Thank You.*

## PRAYER REQUESTS

## PRAISES

## ANSWERS TO PRAYER

## Day 106
# FORGET NOT

My whole being, praise the LORD and do not forget all his kindnesses.
He forgives all my sins and heals all my diseases. He saves my life
from the grave and loads me with love and mercy. He satisfies me
with good things and makes me young again, like the eagle.

PSALM 103:2–5 NCV

*Lord, I will remember Your kindness, Your goodness, and Your love. You have wiped*
*away my past and healed my body and soul. You have given me life never ending,*
*and for that I sing Your praise. You keep me in peace and renew me each day.*

## PRAISES

## PRAYER REQUESTS

## ANSWERS TO PRAYER

# IN THE VALLEY

'Tis the gift to be simple, 'tis the gift to be free,
'Tis the gift to come down where we ought to be—
And when we find ourselves in the place just right,
'Twill be in the valley of love and delight.
SHAKER HYMN

*Heavenly Father, as I read Your Word today, renew my mind. Give me new thinking that is straight from heaven. I love Your truth. Make Your ways known to me; share Your thoughts and plans with me. I delight in You.*

## PRAYER REQUESTS

## PRAISES

## ANSWERS TO PRAYER

# CHERISH

Cherish your visions; cherish your ideals; cherish the music that
stirs in your heart, the beauty that forms in your mind, and the
loveliness that drapes your purest thoughts, for out of them will
grow all delightful conditions, all heavenly environment.

JAMES ALLEN

*Thank You, Lord, for stirring my heart today with worship. I am grateful for the little reminders You bring into my thoughts—a song I haven't sung in years, a memory of Your goodness, the tenderness of Your presence. I am Yours and You are mine.*

## PRAISES

## PRAYER REQUESTS

## ANSWERS TO PRAYER

*Day 109*

# A WELLSPRING OF HOPE

When we suffer, hope still springs up in us. As Christians, we are
especially able to continue anticipating the best, even when life tries
to make us doubt it. Why? Because our hope is firmly set in the God
of all grace, who has already showered us with blessings.

*God, I set my hope on You today. I have an expectation of something good to come.
It burns in me like a white-hot flame. I refuse to let that flame go out. Help me to dismiss
the doubt when it tries to persuade me to believe anything less than the best of You.*

## PRAYER REQUESTS

## ANSWERS TO PRAYER

## PRAISES

# Day 110

## BE ALIVE

Life is what we are alive to. It is not length but breadth. . . .
Be alive. . .to goodness, kindness, purity, love, history,
poetry, music, flowers, stars, God, and eternal hope.
MALTBIE D. BABCOCK

*God, I live for You. Let my life reflect everything good. When I am tempted to dwell on the negative things in my life or in this world, bring me back to the truth. I desire to come alive to the purpose You have for me. Help me point others to You.*

**PRAISES**

**PRAYER REQUESTS**

**ANSWERS TO PRAYER**

# Day 111
## HEALTH VS. MONEY

There is this difference between the two temporal blessings—health and money; money is the most envied, but the least enjoyed; health is the most enjoyed, but the least envied; and this superiority of the latter is still more obvious when we reflect.

CHARLES CALEB COLTON

*Lord, a healthy life is precious and more valuable than money. Yet I find it sometimes tempting to sacrifice my health for wealth, especially when I forget that You are my source for everything I need. Teach me to value You and my health and to trust You for provision.*

.................................................................................................................
.................................................................................................................
.................................................................................................................
.................................................................................................................
.................................................................................................................

### PRAYER REQUESTS

.................................................
.................................................
.................................................
.................................................

### PRAISES

.................................................
.................................................
.................................................
.................................................
.................................................
.................................................
.................................................
.................................................
.................................................
.................................................
.................................................

### ANSWERS TO PRAYER

.................................................
.................................................
.................................................
.................................................

# ACCLAIM HIM!

Blessed are those who have learned to acclaim you,
who walk in the light of your presence, LORD. They rejoice
in your name all day long; they celebrate your righteousness.
PSALM 89:15–16 NIV

*I praise You from the mountaintops to the bottom of the sea. You deserve all the
praise. When I'm tempted to take credit for something, help me to give You the glory
for that accomplishment. I can do nothing without You—and I don't want to.*

........................................................................................................................................

........................................................................................................................................

........................................................................................................................................

........................................................................................................................................

........................................................................................................................................

## PRAISES

## PRAYER REQUESTS

## ANSWERS TO PRAYER

# WILDFLOWER VIRTUES

We complicate our lives when we borrow trouble from the future.
. . . We miss the precious gift of peace that God has given us right
here, right now, in this tiny present moment that touches eternity.
Be like the wildflowers. . .simply soaking up today's sunshine.

ELLYN SANNA

*God, thank You for the gift of peace. When I'm troubled with the what-ifs of tomorrow,
redirect my thoughts to promises. I choose to rest in Your peace today. I trust You
to perfect everything that concerns me. You work all things to my good.*

## PRAYER REQUESTS

## PRAISES

## ANSWERS TO PRAYER

# A SONG AT DAYBREAK

O God, great and wonderful, who has created the heavens, dwelling in the light and beauty thereof; who has made the earth, revealing Yourself in every flower that opens; let not my eyes be blind to You, neither my heart be dead, but teach me to praise You, even as the lark, which offers her song at daybreak.

ISIDORE OF SEVILLE

*Each morning, Lord, I offer praise to You. You give me life and breath each day.*
*I take that to mean that You have something for me to do. Give me a willing heart to*
*do those things as a sacrifice of praise to You, never complaining but always rejoicing.*

## PRAISES

## PRAYER REQUESTS

## ANSWERS TO PRAYER

# PERFECT GIFTS

Don't judge God's gifts until you've unwrapped the whole package. Often His presents are larger than they seem and take longer to unpack than you thought. But in the end, you're likely to learn that whatever pain you put into the situation is much less than His blessing. . . God's gifts are perfect after all.

*Thank You, God, for the unexpected packages You send my way. You know I don't really like surprises, so sometimes I don't respond the way I should. Forgive me. Help me to look at these opportunities to grow in faith, immediately recognizing it's going to be good.*

## PRAYER REQUESTS

## PRAISES

## ANSWERS TO PRAYER

# UNPROMPTED BLESSINGS

God, who is love. . .simply cannot help but shed blessing on blessing
upon us. We do not need to beg, for He simply cannot help it!
HANNAH WHITALL SMITH

*Oh God! Thank You! I am grateful for the shower of blessing You pour out on me.*
*Thank You for Your favor today. When I look to the right or the left, cause bless-*
*ings to overtake me. I bask in the overflow and surrender to Your will for my life.*

## PRAISES

## PRAYER REQUESTS

## ANSWERS TO PRAYER

# Day 117
## THE BEST MOLD

One of God's richest blessings. . .is that our children come
into the world as people we're supposed to guide and direct,
and then God uses them to form us—if we will only listen.

DENA DYER

*God, thank You for the children You've placed in my life. You continue to use them to
teach me new things about You and about myself. Help me to follow You in the way
I am to lead them. Give me grace to receive because I am also learning from them.*

........................................................................................................................

........................................................................................................................

........................................................................................................................

........................................................................................................................

........................................................................................................................

### PRAYER REQUESTS

...............................................................

...............................................................

...............................................................

...............................................................

### ANSWERS TO PRAYER

...............................................................

...............................................................

...............................................................

...............................................................

### PRAISES

...............................................................

...............................................................

...............................................................

...............................................................

...............................................................

...............................................................

...............................................................

...............................................................

...............................................................

...............................................................

...............................................................

# A JOYFUL REWARD

Children are a heritage from the LORD, offspring a reward from him.
Like arrows in the hands of a warrior are children born in one's youth.
PSALM 127:3–4 NIV

*What a beautiful reward You've given me in my sons and daughters. As they grow and mature, my world completely changes. Help me to appreciate the gift they are to me in every season of our lives. And may I always honor You in mentoring them.*

.........................................................................................................................................
.........................................................................................................................................
.........................................................................................................................................
.........................................................................................................................................
.........................................................................................................................................

## PRAISES

## PRAYER REQUESTS

## ANSWERS TO PRAYER

# SPECIAL DELIVERIES

God sends children. . .to enlarge our hearts, to make us unselfish and full of
kindly sympathies and affections, to give our souls higher aims. . .to bring
round our fireside bright faces and happy smiles, and loving, tender hearts.
MARY HOWITT

*God, my heart grew larger with each child You gave me. From those born to me
to those You choose for me to raise spiritually, I love each one differently. Help
me to hear from heaven for each one as individually as You have made us.*

## PRAYER REQUESTS

## PRAISES

## ANSWERS TO PRAYER

## *Day 120*
# CHOOSE TO REJOICE

It is no use to grumble and complain;  It's just as cheap and easy to rejoice;
When God sorts out the weather and sends rain—Why, rain's my choice.
JAMES WHITCOMB RILEY

*God, I always regret my words after I have complained. It doesn't just steal my joy; it is a thief in the hearts of those I speak negative words to. Tap me on the heart when I am tempted to complain. Help me to add to the lives of others with positive, loving words.*

## PRAISES

## PRAYER REQUESTS

## ANSWERS TO PRAYER

# NORMAL DAY

Normal day, let me be aware of the treasure you are. Let me
learn from you, love you, bless you before you depart. Let me
not pass you by in quest of some rare and perfect tomorrow.

MARY JEAN IRION

*It's tempting to live each day pressing for tomorrow. Give me patience and peace to live
in the moment. Open my eyes to see the blessing today truly is. Just a normal day can
be precious and valuable when I spend it with You. Help me to cherish normal days.*

......................................................................................................................................................................

......................................................................................................................................................................

......................................................................................................................................................................

......................................................................................................................................................................

## PRAYER REQUESTS

......................................................................................

......................................................................................

......................................................................................

......................................................................................

## PRAISES

......................................................................................

......................................................................................

......................................................................................

......................................................................................

......................................................................................

......................................................................................

......................................................................................

......................................................................................

......................................................................................

......................................................................................

## ANSWERS TO PRAYER

......................................................................................

......................................................................................

......................................................................................

......................................................................................

# Day 122
## SEEK WISDOM

*Lord, thank You for the gift of physical pleasures, but teach us to use them wisely, according to Your will. Keep us faithful to our husbands and to Your laws of self-control. Thank You for the life I enjoy. The simple pleasures of good food and entertainment are a gift. But too much of a good thing can lead to a mundane life. Forgive me for unintentionally vegging out, leaning into procrastination, or giving in to an unproductive cycle in my life.*

### PRAISES

### PRAYER REQUESTS

### ANSWERS TO PRAYER

## Day 123

# A UNITED HOUSEHOLD

May [God] grant you all the things which your heart desires, and may [He] give you a [spouse] and a home and gracious concord, for there is nothing greater and better than this—when a husband and wife keep a household in oneness of mind, a great woe to their enemies and joy to their friends, and win high renown.

HOMER

*God, there are many reasons I argue with my husband. It's so hard when we're not on the same page. Sometimes we are saying the same thing, and we don't even realize it. Help me to be a clear communicator in my home. Be the center of each conversation.*

## PRAYER REQUESTS

## PRAISES

## ANSWERS TO PRAYER

# NEVER SEPARATED

For I am convinced that neither death nor life, neither angels nor
demons, neither the present nor the future, nor any powers, neither
height nor depth, nor anything else in all creation, will be able to
separate us from the love of God that is in Christ Jesus our Lord.

ROMANS 8:38–39 NIV

*The truth that nothing can separate me from Your love is powerful. Never
have I experienced a love like Yours anywhere. Thank You for loving me,
embracing me, and understanding me in a way no one else does.*

## PRAISES

## PRAYER REQUESTS

## ANSWERS TO PRAYER

# Day 125
## NATURAL WONDERS

The wonder of living is held within the beauty of silence, the glory
of sunlight, the sweetness of fresh spring air, the quiet strength of
earth, and the love that lies at the very root of all things.

Unknown

*Father, I cannot fathom the love You have for me. You have gone to great lengths to
demonstrate Your love. Thank You for loving me when I was lost and didn't know
You. Your love called to me, beckoning me to come home to Your awaiting arms.*

...............................................................................................................
...............................................................................................................
...............................................................................................................
...............................................................................................................
...............................................................................................................

## PRAYER REQUESTS

...............................................................................
...............................................................................
...............................................................................
...............................................................................

## PRAISES

...............................................................................
...............................................................................
...............................................................................
...............................................................................
...............................................................................
...............................................................................
...............................................................................
...............................................................................
...............................................................................

## ANSWERS TO PRAYER

...............................................................................
...............................................................................
...............................................................................
...............................................................................

# INEXHAUSTIBLE RICHES

God's richness is such that He can totally give Himself to every man, can be there only for him—and likewise for a second and third, for millions and thousands of millions. That is the mystery of his infinity and inexhaustible richness.

LADISLAUS BOROS

*God, thank You for giving Yourself to every person, something very hard for us to understand. You are the Almighty One, able to do the miraculous. Thank You for Your rich mercy and love at work in me.*

## PRAISES

## PRAYER REQUESTS

## ANSWERS TO PRAYER

# Day 127

## HIS MARVELOUS CREATION

Have you ever looked at God's stars and marveled as they lit the velvet-dark sky? Watched a sunset in which the sky was tinted from the lightest blue on the horizon to a deep tone above and delighted in God's paintbrush? Then you've seen Him make things beautiful in their time.

*I look back and see how You have made the things in my life, once ugly and decaying, beautiful and alive again. Over the season of my life, You have masterfully crafted me into Your image. Forgive me when I've resisted. Please continue to mold and make me even now.*

...................................................................................................................
...................................................................................................................
...................................................................................................................
...................................................................................................................
...................................................................................................................

### PRAYER REQUESTS

......................................................
......................................................
......................................................
......................................................

### ANSWERS TO PRAYER

......................................................
......................................................
......................................................
......................................................

### PRAISES

......................................................
......................................................
......................................................
......................................................
......................................................
......................................................
......................................................
......................................................
......................................................
......................................................
......................................................

## Day 128

# HIS UNFAILING LOVE

"Though the mountains be shaken and the hills be removed, yet my unfailing love for you will not be shaken nor my covenant of peace be removed," says the LORD, who has compassion on you.

ISAIAH 54:10 NIV

*Thank You, Lord, for Your promises that cannot be broken. Your Word is forever true and Your faithfulness unending. In those moments when the circumstances of life try to shake my foundation, Your covenant keeps me grounded to You. I hold tight to Your unfailing love.*

### PRAISES

### PRAYER REQUESTS

### ANSWERS TO PRAYER

# Day 129
## MAY

The word *May* is a perfumed word. . . . It means youth,
love, song, and all that is beautiful in life.
HENRY WADSWORTH LONGFELLOW

*Your promises are yes and amen in my life. And I choose to embrace Your love and
everything a relationship with You brings. Restore my youth with Your love. Thank You
for singing songs of deliverance over me and setting me on a beautiful path to You.*

## PRAYER REQUESTS

## PRAISES

## ANSWERS TO PRAYER

## Day 130
# TAKE HEART

"Blessed are you when people hate you, when they exclude you and insult you and reject your name as evil, because of the Son of Man."
LUKE 6:22 NIV

*When I am persecuted for Your name's sake, remind me that Jesus lived a counterculture in His time on earth. He went against the flow and followed the Father's will no matter what others said to Him or about Him. I will stand firm in the face of insult because I choose Your side.*

### PRAISES

### PRAYER REQUESTS

### ANSWERS TO PRAYER

## Day 131

# A SONG OF THANKSGIVING

*You bless my life in many ways every day, Father. May I receive Your blessings with a song of thanksgiving on my lips. Father, let the words of my mouth and the meditations of my heart please You. Each time I open my mouth, let thanksgiving flow. I am grateful to You, God. Everything I have I owe to You. You have given me precious gifts for which I am eternally grateful.*

## PRAYER REQUESTS

## ANSWERS TO PRAYER

## PRAISES

## Day 132

# SIMPLE BLESSINGS

To find the universal elements enough; to find the air and water
exhilarating; to be refreshed by a morning walk or an evening saunter
. . .to be thrilled by the stars at night; to be elated over a bird's nest or a
wildflower in spring—these are some of the rewards of the simple life.

JOHN BURROUGHS

*God, I see Your majesty in the roar of the ocean, Your strength in the thunderclouds. I am
reminded of Your great love as the sea kisses the sand. Whisper to me in the gentle breeze,
and embrace me with the comfort of a summer rain. All of creation speaks Your name.*

## PRAISES

## PRAYER REQUESTS

## ANSWERS TO PRAYER

# NEVER LACKING

God's goodness and mercy come in many packages and many sizes, but they follow us each day of our existence. Whether we've passed through many hard times or just a few, no day given to any believer following Jesus lacks these two blessings.

*You are my source, Lord. Your Word promises I will never lack any good thing because I belong to You. Your goodness and mercy will follow me all the days of my life. I choose to live for You and bring You glory in all I do.*

## PRAYER REQUESTS

## PRAISES

## ANSWERS TO PRAYER

# NO ACCIDENTS

Nothing hurts so much as dissatisfaction with our circumstances. . . .
God knows what He is doing, and there is nothing accidental in the life
of the believer. Nothing but good can come to those who are wholly His.
WATCHMAN NEE

*God, when things don't go my way and I suffer disappointment, help me to pause. In
that moment, take me back in my mind to the times You've turned things around to
bring me something better than I imagined. And this time I'll trust You to do it again.*

## PRAISES

## PRAYER REQUESTS

## ANSWERS TO PRAYER

# *Day 135*
## SMALL PLEASURES

Happiness consists more in small conveniences or pleasures
that occur every day than in the great pieces of good fortune
that happen but seldom to a man in the course of his life.
BENJAMIN FRANKLIN

*Lord, help me to treasure the little moments that bring a smile to my face and a bubble
of joy to my soul. It's the little things every day that steady my course and confirm Your
hand is on my life. Point me gently in the right direction, and I will always follow.*

PRAYER REQUESTS

PRAISES

ANSWERS TO PRAYER

# Day 136
## FILLED WITH LAUGHTER

Our mouths were filled with laughter, our tongues with songs of joy. Then
it was said among the nations, "The LORD has done great things for them."
The LORD has done great things for us, and we are filled with joy.
PSALM 126:2–3 NIV

*Let laughter take me to a new place in You. As I savor those precious moments when
my soul overflows, join me in this little celebration. You are my joy and the lifter of
my head. Thank You for putting these precious little nuggets of joy in my day.*

### PRAISES

### PRAYER REQUESTS

### ANSWERS TO PRAYER

## Day 137

# WE THANK THEE

For health and food, for love and friends, for everything
Thy goodness sends, Father in Heaven, we thank Thee.
RALPH WALDO EMERSON

*Father, I am so thankful for all You have done in my life. You have saved me more times*
*than I can count. You've comforted me in seasons of grief. You've celebrated every*
*single joyful moment of my life. May my heart forever overflow with gratitude to You.*

......................................................................................................................................................
......................................................................................................................................................
......................................................................................................................................................
......................................................................................................................................................
......................................................................................................................................................
......................................................................................................................................................

### PRAYER REQUESTS

......................................................
......................................................
......................................................
......................................................

### PRAISES

......................................................
......................................................
......................................................
......................................................
......................................................
......................................................
......................................................
......................................................
......................................................
......................................................

### ANSWERS TO PRAYER

......................................................
......................................................
......................................................
......................................................

# FAMILY GIFTS

Families give us many things—love and meaning,
purpose and an opportunity to give, and a sense of humor.

UNKNOWN

*Father, thank You for my family—the ones who are easy to love and the ones who challenge me. Although I didn't choose my family, You did! Give me a deep love and compassion for each one of them. Teach me to live my life in a way that points them to You.*

## PRAISES

## PRAYER REQUESTS

## ANSWERS TO PRAYER

# Day 139
## HIS CHILD

You are God's child. That might seem a rather ordinary thing, but consider it more carefully, and feel the amazement of that truth. The Creator of the universe, the all-powerful God, wants to be your daddy (after all, that's what *abba* means). This awesome being wants you to trust Him and seek His love and protection.

*Father, sometimes it's hard to see You as my Father. Help me to under-stand what that means. Give me moments with You where I feel like a child who can crawl up in Your lap and just rest. Help me to hear Your voice of encouragement. May my choices bring You glory.*

### PRAYER REQUESTS

### PRAISES

### ANSWERS TO PRAYER

# NO FEAR

We walk without fear, full of hope and courage and strength to
do His will, waiting for the endless good which He is always
giving as fast as He can get us able to take it in.
Geoarge MacDonald

*Lord, I am waiting for Your endless good. But in between now and then,
may I live each day full of hope that comes from You. Make me courageous and powered by Your strength to do all that You have asked
of me. Grow my capacity to receive more of Your good today.*

## PRAISES

## PRAYER REQUESTS

## ANSWERS TO PRAYER

## Day 141
# LESS IS MORE

Fear less, hope more; eat less, chew more; whine less, breathe more;
talk less, say more; hate less, love more, and all good things are yours.
SWEDISH PROVERB

*God, thank You for the opportunity to choose Your good in this life. Today I
ask You to help me trust You more, expect more of Your grace, and love with
a greater capacity. Help me to become more of who You created me to be.*

## PRAYER REQUESTS

## PRAISES

## ANSWERS TO PRAYER

## *Day 142*
# FROM ABOVE

Every good and perfect gift is from above, coming down from the Father
of the heavenly lights, who does not change like shifting shadows.
JAMES 1:17 NIV

*Thank You, heavenly Father, for being so dependable. You never change. Your Word
stands true from generation to generation. I trust You to remain faithful every step of
my journey. Give me wisdom to always stay close to You, forever in Your perfect will.*

## PRAISES

## PRAYER REQUESTS

## ANSWERS TO PRAYER

# FOCUS ON THE PRESENT

*Lord, help me to rejoice in the time I have with my family today. I don't want to dwell on what might happen in the future; I want to relish this chance to nurture and cherish the blessings You've given me. Lord, sometimes family relationships are hard. I know You understand. Give me wisdom, understanding, and a heart to hear what others have to say. Help me to discern what is good and acceptable to You and what I should let go. Show me how to love my family like You do.*

## PRAYER REQUESTS

## PRAISES

## ANSWERS TO PRAYER

# GIVE LOVE

Love is the greatest thing that God can give us; for He Himself
is love; and it is the greatest thing we can give to God.

JEREMY TAYLOR

*God, thank You for loving me unconditionally. Show me how to accept Your love.
Help me to demonstrate to others how much You love them. Give me compassion to love others the way You do. Give me patience when doing that is hard.*

## PRAISES

## PRAYER REQUESTS

## ANSWERS TO PRAYER

# OUR HEAVENLY WEATHERMAN

The weather is not ours but God's to control. We need to give thanks
for the daily blessings God offers us—rain that keeps wells and
reservoirs filled or sunshine for a special outing. When the weather
doesn't go "our way," we can still thank God that He's in control.

*Father, I'm always quick to thank You for the beautiful days filled with sunshine and
beauty. Forgive me for complaining when it's drab and dreary, especially in the rainy
season. I am grateful for all the seasons You've given me, because I need all of them.*

## PRAYER REQUESTS

## PRAISES

## ANSWERS TO PRAYER

# GOD IS GOOD

The merry birds prolong the strain, their song with every spring renewed;
and balmy air, and falling rain, each softly whispers: God is good.
JOHN HAMPDEN GURNEY

*Help me, Lord, to slow down and give thanks for the birds that sing. My life is often so busy, I seldom notice their songs. But You put their music on this earth to bring me joy. So remind me to treasure the quiet moments and appreciate the songs the birds sing.*

## PRAISES

## PRAYER REQUESTS

## ANSWERS TO PRAYER

# COMMON MIRACLES

The miracles of nature do not seem miraculous because they
are so common. If no one had ever seen a flower, even a
dandelion would be the most startling event in the world.

UNKNOWN

*I never want to take Your miracles for granted. May I see the flowers that grow in
the desert places and appreciate the beauty of the majestic mountains. Give me a
deep appreciation for the glorious creation You created for me. Thank You, Lord.*

## PRAYER REQUESTS

## PRAISES

## ANSWERS TO PRAYER

# Day 148

## BLESSED ARE YOU

"Blessed are the poor in spirit, for theirs is the kingdom of heaven.
Blessed are those who mourn, for they shall be comforted. Blessed
are the meek, for they shall inherit the earth. Blessed are those who
hunger and thirst for righteousness, for they shall be satisfied."
MATTHEW 5:3–6 ESV

*Thank You for the blessings You have so graciously given to me. When I turn to the left
or the right, Your grace and mercy meet me. Whatever I need, You have already provided. You stand before me with an open hand, ready to give me whatever I need.*

........................................................................................................................
........................................................................................................................
........................................................................................................................
........................................................................................................................
........................................................................................................................

| PRAISES | PRAYER REQUESTS |
|---|---|
| | |

| | ANSWERS TO PRAYER |
|---|---|
| | |

# FIND A PATH

The means by which different people are led and in which they find the blessing of God are varied, transposed, and combined together a thousand different ways.
JOHN WESLEY

*Heavenly Father, thank You for leading me individually and for speaking to me specifically. Your gospel is specific and precise for my life. You have set a path before me that You've called me to pursue. Thank You that it doesn't always look like everyone else's.*

## PRAYER REQUESTS

## PRAISES

## ANSWERS TO PRAYER

# A SENSE OF BEAUTIFUL

A man should hear a little music, read a little poetry, and see a fine picture every day of his life, in order that worldly cares may not obliterate the sense of the beautiful which God has implanted in the human soul.

JOHANN WOLFGANG VON GOETHE

*Thank You for the gifts and talents You've placed inside of me. I appreciate the simple joys that sing a song You've written just for my heartstrings. Don't let me miss a single moment of beauty that You prepared for my soul to see.*

## PRAISES

## PRAYER REQUESTS

## ANSWERS TO PRAYER

# Day 151
## EXCELLENT THINGS!

Excellent things! God doesn't just do good things or the best things. He does excellent things. What could improve on God's superb plan or will? Are our eyes open to the excellent things He's done for His people—and is still doing for them today?

*God, You do excellent things. Sometimes I'm looking in the wrong direction and miss them. Open my eyes to see the excellent things You are doing in me, around me, and through those I love. Use me to bring You glory in the lives of others.*

### PRAYER REQUESTS

### PRAISES

### ANSWERS TO PRAYER

# Day 152
## AWESOME LANDSCAPES

*Dear Lord, we give You thanks for the bright silent moon, and thanks for the sun that will warm us at noon. And thanks for the stars and the quick running breeze, and thanks for the shade and straightness of trees. Lord, help me to pause. I need to take time more often to see the spectacular world You created for me to enjoy. I will stop and look around when those opportunities come my way. I will not be too busy. I will take a deep breath and appreciate Your beauty.*

### PRAISES

### PRAYER REQUESTS

### ANSWERS TO PRAYER

# INCOMPREHENSIBLE LOVE

We are so preciously loved by God that we cannot even comprehend it. No created being can ever know how much and how sweetly and tenderly God loves them.

JULIAN OF NORWICH

*God, it's hard to imagine it, but I know it's true—no one loves me more than You. I love my family deeply, but You love them more than I ever could. Even though I can't fathom the depth of Your love, I accept that You love much more than I could ever know how.*

## PRAYER REQUESTS

## ANSWERS TO PRAYER

## PRAISES

# HIS BELOVED EARTH

You care for the land and water it; you enrich it abundantly.
The streams of God are filled with water to provide the people
with grain, for so you have ordained it. You drench its furrows
and level its ridges; you soften it with showers and bless its crops.

PSALM 65:9–10 NIV

*Help me, Lord, to be a good steward of the land You've given me, the water
You've provided, and the provision You've put in my life. I am thankful not to
waste it or take any of it for granted. It is all a gift from You. Thank You.*

## PRAISES

## PRAYER REQUESTS

## ANSWERS TO PRAYER

## Day 155

# IN HIS FOOTSTEPS

When someone does a kindness, it always seems to me
That's the way God up in heaven would like us all to be.
For when we. . .have followed in His footsteps. . .I'm very sure it's true
That in serving those around us, we serve and please God too.
HELEN STEINER RICE

*Remind me that Your blessings are not given for what I've done. They are gifts because of Your great love. May I never withhold a blessing to someone because of how I feel or think about that. May I always open my hand and give to others just as You've given to me.*

## PRAYER REQUESTS

## PRAISES

## ANSWERS TO PRAYER

# TIME

Let me tell thee, time is a very precious gift of God;
so precious that it's only given to us moment by moment.
AMELIA BARR

~

*Thank You, God, for the time You've given me. I pray I will use it to bring You joy
and pleasure. May I also not feel guilty for taking time to rest and enjoy the life
You've given me. Help me to treasure the simple moments and not hurry too much.*

......................................................................................................................

......................................................................................................................

......................................................................................................................

......................................................................................................................

......................................................................................................................

......................................................................................................................

## PRAISES

## PRAYER REQUESTS

## ANSWERS TO PRAYER

## Day 157

# OUR NEEDS FULFILLED

God's blessings begin with the spiritual, but they don't end there. As God recognizes the needs of this world, we should too. Often, it's the body's needs that make people aware of spiritual emptiness. God deals with every phase of our lives, and as we offer Jesus to others, we can do that too.

*God, You are all I need. I am complete in You. Your Word says You will supply all my needs. Thank You for prospering my soul as I lean into You. Fill my heart with Your compassion for others to know and experience You as well.*

### PRAYER REQUESTS

### PRAISES

### ANSWERS TO PRAYER

*Day 158*

# OPEN YOUR HEART

The best and most beautiful things in the world cannot
be seen nor even touched, but just felt in the heart.
HELEN KELLER

*Heavenly Father, sometimes I shut my eyes and my heart to the cruelty and ugliness of this world. It's easier not to look. But I know I need to respond with a heart like Yours. So help me to open my heart to see things like You so that I see the beautiful things too.*

........................................................................................................................

........................................................................................................................

........................................................................................................................

........................................................................................................................

........................................................................................................................

........................................................................................................................

## PRAISES

## PRAYER REQUESTS

## ANSWERS TO PRAYER

## *Day 159*
# OVERFLOWING BEAUTY

The full woods overflow among the meadow's gold! A bluebell wave
has rolled, where crowded cowslips grow. The drifting hawthorn snow
brims over hill and world. The full woods overflow among the meadow's
gold. . . . Heaven's beauty crowds below, the full woods overflow!

MARY WEBB

*Thank You, Lord, for this beautiful world. When I take time to walk in Your creation,
I am amazed by You. I feel closer to You as I breathe in the majestic miracles of all You
have made. I am grateful that You created me in Your image and I belong to You.*

## PRAYER REQUESTS

## PRAISES

## ANSWERS TO PRAYER

# Day 160
## GOD'S PLAN

And this is God's plan: Both Gentiles and Jews who believe the Good News share equally in the riches inherited by God's children. Both are part of the same body, and both enjoy the promise of blessings because they belong to Christ Jesus.
EPHESIANS 3:6 NLT

*Heavenly Father, thank You for including all people in Your eternal plan. Help me to value people by nothing other than the way You see them. You love every single one of us and desire that all may come to know You personally. Give me opportunities to lead others to You.*

### PRAISES

### PRAYER REQUESTS

### ANSWERS TO PRAYER

# Day 161

## FINDING THE GOOD

You may tend to think of God gratefully in the good times and ask
for His help in the bad. But sometimes you have to consider that
God brings good out of both. No matter what your feelings tell you,
you can trust Him to work out His purpose in you at all times.

*God, not matter how I feel or what the circumstances of my life seem like, You are always
good. You have a path set for me, and I choose to walk in it. As I travel through it, I trust
You will bring me to the places I need to traverse and ultimately use my life for Your good.*

.......................................................................................
.......................................................................................
.......................................................................................
.......................................................................................
.......................................................................................

### PRAYER REQUESTS

### PRAISES

### ANSWERS TO PRAYER

## Day 162
# BLESSED SECURITY

*Lord, I thank You for Your guidance and protection day after day. Although I never know what the day will bring, You have a plan, and I trust in You. Holy Spirit, I am listening. Lead me and I will follow You. I am always in the right place at the right time to bring glory to the Father. He leads me and protects me. He has a plan and a purpose and both of them are good. Thank You that my best days are just ahead.*

## PRAISES

## PRAYER REQUESTS

## ANSWERS TO PRAYER

# *Day 163*

## YOURS FOR THE TAKING

It's for you I created the universe [says God]. I love you. There's only one catch. Like any other gift, the gift of grace can be yours only if you'll reach out and take it. Maybe being able to reach out and take it is a gift too.

FREDERICK BUECHNER

*Thank You, God, for the good gifts You give. I am grateful for Your grace. Without Your grace I would not be who I am today. You have forgiven me and poured out Your favor on me. I receive Your blessing of grace in my life. I reach out and take it today. What a beautiful gift.*

### PRAYER REQUESTS

### PRAISES

### ANSWERS TO PRAYER

## Day 164

# NO MORE YEARNING

In all ranks of life the human heart yearns for the beautiful;
and the beautiful things that God makes are His gift to all alike.

HARRIET BEECHER STOWE

*You make beautiful things. Nothing you have created is without majesty, grandeur,*
*and worth. Thank You for taking something broken like my life and making me new.*
*I am forever grateful for Your handiwork to repair, restore, and renew my life.*

........................................................................................................

........................................................................................................

........................................................................................................

........................................................................................................

........................................................................................................

........................................................................................................

## PRAISES

## PRAYER REQUESTS

## ANSWERS TO PRAYER

# Day 165
## HUMOR

Humor is the great thing, the saving thing, after all. The minute
it crops up, all our hardnesses yield, all our irritations and
resentments flit away, and a sunny spirit takes their place.
MARK TWAIN

*Father, thank You for the gift of humor. Laughter erases the stress and removes
the pain, if only for a moment. Laughter lifts my spirit and breaks the tension
in relationships. May I not take myself so seriously all the time. This life
is only a moment in time when compared to the eternity with You.*

## PRAYER REQUESTS

## PRAISES

## ANSWERS TO PRAYER

## Day 166

# GOD BLESS YOU

"The LORD bless you and keep you; the LORD make His face shine upon you, and be gracious to you; the LORD lift up His countenance upon you, and give you peace."
NUMBERS 6:24–26 NKJV

*I hold those I know and love before You, Lord. May You bless each one with Your joy, Your favor, and Your healing. Speak to their hearts so that they may come to know You and realize the gift You have extended to them to spend eternity with You, starting now.*

........................................................................................................

........................................................................................................

........................................................................................................

........................................................................................................

........................................................................................................

### PRAISES

### PRAYER REQUESTS

### ANSWERS TO PRAYER

## Day 167
# REST ASSURED

Rest is not idleness, and to lie sometimes on the grass under trees on a summer's day, listening to the murmur of water, or watching the clouds float across the sky, is by no means a waste of time.

SIR JOHN LUBBOCK

*Lord, Your Word encourages me to plan seasons of rest. Sometimes I find it hard to stop and rest. Help me to schedule that time each day and to take time off from the stress of this life to put my feet up and breathe. Show me how to teach my family the importance of leisure.*

PRAYER REQUESTS

PRAISES

ANSWERS TO PRAYER

# Day 168
## RELAX!

God provides resting places as well as working places. Rest, then,
and be thankful when he brings you, wearied to a wayside well.
L. B. COWMAN

*Thank You, Lord, for the work You give me. I am grateful to put my
hand to the plow so that I may have seed to sow into the kingdom of
God. You have promised what I put my hand to will prosper. Each gift
I give is a blessing, and You will return it to me on every wave.*

| PRAISES |
| --- |
|  |
|  |
|  |
|  |
|  |
|  |
|  |
|  |
|  |

| PRAYER REQUESTS |
| --- |
|  |
|  |
|  |
|  |

| ANSWERS TO PRAYER |
| --- |
|  |
|  |
|  |

# Day 169
## FAMILY TIME

*Thank You for my home, dear Jesus. I just love to be here. I can't explain the joy that comes from being surrounded by those I love. Whether our home is filled with laughter during game night or shrouded in silent contemplation during family devotions, I can feel Your presence, and I am uplifted. I pray that all who enter my home are greeted with Your peace and Your presence. May they know You reside here. May Your love and compassion fill this house. Let our relationships add to our life, and may each word spoken be a blessing to another.*

### PRAYER REQUESTS

### ANSWERS TO PRAYER

### PRAISES

# UNCUT DIAMONDS

Guard well your spare moments. They are like uncut diamonds.
Discard them and their value will never be known. Improve them
and they will become the brightest gems in a useful life.

RALPH WALDO EMERSON

*Lord, my life is but a grain of sand in the sea of time. Please help me to
make the most of every moment. I don't want to get caught in the trap
of things that truly won't matter a lifetime from now. Give me peace to
pursue the season of my life and find what is most valuable.*

## PRAISES

## PRAYER REQUESTS

## ANSWERS TO PRAYER

# Day 171
## A LIGHT IN THE DARK

For many people, the heavy responsibilities of home and family and earning a living absorb all their time and strength. Yet such a home—where love is—may be a light shining in a dark place, a silent witness to the reality and love of God.

OLIVE WYON

*God, just like we leave the porch light on for friends and family coming into our home, I thank You that my heart light is always on to shine the light of Your love to be a witness to those who find themselves in the dark. Help me to bring them to Your light.*

PRAYER REQUESTS

PRAISES

ANSWERS TO PRAYER

## *Day 172*
# LITTLE IN RETURN

He has shown you, O mortal, what is good. And what does the LORD require
of you? To act justly and to love mercy and to walk humbly with your God.
MICAH 6:8 NIV

*Lord, help me to stay humble. Whatever I accomplish in this life is only because of Your
blessing. All I have You provided. May I always respond in love, with mercy toward others,
seeking justice. When I think more of myself than I should, remind me who You are.*

PRAISES

PRAYER REQUESTS

ANSWERS TO PRAYER

# Day 173
## FRIENDS ARE A GIFT

*Dear God, thank You for my friends. Help me not to take them for granted. . . .*
*Remind me often how poor my life would be without the friends You've given me.*
*Help me to enrich their lives as they have mine. Dear God, relationships with*
*those You put in my life are the most important part of who You created me to*
*be. We need one another. Never let me lose sight of that. May I always be will-*
*ing to put others first and never take advantage of the love they have for me.*

### PRAYER REQUESTS

### ANSWERS TO PRAYER

### PRAISES

# GOOD FRIENDS

It is not part of God's plan that each one of us has beauty or fame. But believe
He did intend for all of us to know the kindness and compassion of a friend.

ANITA WIEGARD

*God, thank You for the many reasons I have to celebrate, especially the good You've pro-vided to those I know and love. May I never covet what they have or wish them a negative thought. Fill me with great compassion for Your people. May I love them like You do.*

## PRAISES

## PRAYER REQUESTS

## ANSWERS TO PRAYER

# Day 175
## OUR MISSION

By placing us in this world, God has given us a mission, and prayer is a part of it. By lifting others up to Him, we take part in the blessing He bestows upon the world. Just as Jesus won't forget us, we need to remember those whose lives we touch. Because we know Jesus, we can pray effectively— and perhaps that's the most potent impact we'll have on another's life.

*Forgive me, Father, for the times I said I would pray for someone and didn't. Give me courage to step up and apply my faith in every circumstance. When someone asks me to pray, prompt me to pray right then. Speak to me and through me as I lift that person to You.*

......................................................................................................................

......................................................................................................................

......................................................................................................................

......................................................................................................................

......................................................................................................................

### PRAYER REQUESTS

......................................................

......................................................

......................................................

......................................................

### PRAISES

......................................................

......................................................

......................................................

......................................................

......................................................

......................................................

......................................................

......................................................

......................................................

......................................................

### ANSWERS TO PRAYER

......................................................

......................................................

......................................................

......................................................

# THE LESSON OF PAIN

How little we know what God has in store
As daily He blesses our lives more and more. . . .
For pain has a way of broadening our view
And bringing us closer in sympathy too. . . .
So thank You, God, for the gift You sent
To teach me that pain's heaven-sent.

HELEN STEINER RICE

*Thank You, Father, that You will use pain to stretch my faith, to show me Your faithfulness, and to help me realize that I can always depend on You.*

## PRAISES

## PRAYER REQUESTS

## ANSWERS TO PRAYER

# AN INHABITED GARDEN

The world is so empty if one thinks only of mountains,
rivers and cities; but to know someone here and there who
thinks and feels with us, and who, though distant, is close to
us in spirit, this makes the earth for us an inhabited garden.

JOHANN WOLFGANG VON GOETHE

*Thank you, Father, for those who have gone before me, who have experi-
enced the same circumstances I am enduring, so that I can benefit from
their faith. Let me lean into the lessons that they have learned and glean
wisdom from them so that my own challenges are better overcome.*

## PRAYER REQUESTS

## PRAISES

## ANSWERS TO PRAYER

# BLESS OTHERS

God has given each of you a gift. Use it to help
each other. This will show God's loving-favor.
1 PETER 4:10 NLV

*God, the little light of mine that You have provided to my soul, I will
shine for You. Give me strength to never hide it from those who need
it, no matter how dark the night. When I have an experience that will
help, may I tell it to others so they may find their way to You.*

## PRAISES

## PRAYER REQUESTS

## ANSWERS TO PRAYER

# Day 179
## GIFT OF FRIENDSHIP

Blessed are they who have the gift of making friends, for it is one of God's
best gifts. It involves many things, but above all the power of going out
of one's self and appreciating what is noble and loving in another.

THOMAS HUGHES

*God, I am so grateful for those You have placed in my life. Thank You for those who
speak the truth in love, pray for me, stand in faith with me, and encourage me when
things get hard. Show me how I can love them more and be a blessing to them.*

.......................................................................................................................................
.......................................................................................................................................
.......................................................................................................................................
.......................................................................................................................................
.......................................................................................................................................

### PRAYER REQUESTS

.......................................................................................
.......................................................................................
.......................................................................................
.......................................................................................

### PRAISES

.......................................................................................
.......................................................................................
.......................................................................................
.......................................................................................
.......................................................................................
.......................................................................................
.......................................................................................
.......................................................................................
.......................................................................................
.......................................................................................
.......................................................................................

### ANSWERS TO PRAYER

.......................................................................................
.......................................................................................
.......................................................................................

## Day 180
# FAITHFUL COMPANIONSHIP

*Dear God, thank You for understanding friends. Thank You that so often we're on the same wavelength, laughing together, crying together, encouraging each other with our understanding. I'm grateful that I'm not alone, that I can share my life with my friends. Let me never forget that they are there. May I never believe the lie that they are too busy to listen or take time to care. They are here for me just as You are. When I am struggling, help me to reach out and ask them for their support with authenticity.*

### PRAISES

### PRAYER REQUESTS

### ANSWERS TO PRAYER

# WE'RE NEVER LOST

God's blessings are available to even the most disobedient child who turns from sin. Pray for that loved one to turn and accept the Savior's love. Over and over God gave that blessing to Israel. He'll give it to those you love too.

*Dear Father, You know the very one I am praying for right now. You love them more than I ever could, and I love them with my whole heart. Watch over them; protect and keep them. Bring them near to You so that they may surrender all to You.*

## PRAYER REQUESTS

## PRAISES

## ANSWERS TO PRAYER

# A PRETTY GOOD WORLD

Take one thing with another, and the world is a pretty good sort
of world, and it is our duty to make the best of it and be thankful.
BENJAMIN FRANKLIN

⌒

*God, thank You for our world. Admittedly, we haven't taken very good care of it.*
*Forgive us. I am grateful to be alive today and able to stand in faith and intercede on*
*behalf of all who don't know You. Help us make the best of what You've given us.*

.......................................................................................................................................

.......................................................................................................................................

.......................................................................................................................................

.......................................................................................................................................

.......................................................................................................................................

.......................................................................................................................................

.......................................................................................................................................

## PRAISES

## PRAYER REQUESTS

## ANSWERS TO PRAYER

# Day 183
## YOUTHFUL JOY

When the voices of children are heard on the green,
And laughing is heard on the hill,
My heart is at rest within my breast,
And everything else is still.
WILLIAM BLAKE

*Thank You, Lord, for children. Remind me to have childlike faith and to take each moment as it comes like I did when I was still a child. May the laughter of a child always be with me. I will pause, give thanks, and remember the goodness of today.*

## PRAYER REQUESTS

## PRAISES

## ANSWERS TO PRAYER

# Day 184

# AN OUTPOURING OF BLESSING

"For I will pour water on the thirsty land, and streams on the dry ground;
I will pour my Spirit upon your offspring, and my blessing on your descendants."
ISAIAH 44:3 ESV

*God, pour Your spirit on my flesh. I am thirsty for You. Water me with Your
presence, and wash me with Your truth. Fill my soul with everything good so
that I may share it with others and pass it on to the next generation.*

## PRAISES

## PRAYER REQUESTS

## ANSWERS TO PRAYER

## Day 185
# HE IS ALWAYS NEAR

What other nation is so great as to have their gods near them
the way the LORD our God is near us whenever we pray to him?
DEUTERONOMY 4:7 NIV

*Lord, You are near to me. You are always with me. I am so thankful that I don't
have to travel far to be in Your presence or jump through hoops to get You to respond
to me. Help me to be attentive to Your voice and obedient to Your commands.*

## PRAYER REQUESTS

## PRAISES

## ANSWERS TO PRAYER

# SMALL WONDERS

Everything has its wonders, even darkness and silence,
and I learn, whatever state I may be in, therein to be content.
HELEN KELLER

*God, I have times in my life when I really struggle to be content. I want to fix things,
to control outcomes, or just to know how it will all end. But today, I choose to rest in
You. You are my helper. I trust You to perfect all that concerns me in Your time.*

## PRAISES

## PRAYER REQUESTS

## ANSWERS TO PRAYER

# NOTHING UNAPPRECIATED

God doesn't promise to give all we want in a moment. The Christian walk is one of asking, seeking, knocking. God wants us to value the gifts He gives, and anything received too easily is also easily despised. Though He gives wholeheartedly and offers only the best, Jesus will have nothing unappreciated.

*Jesus, I am so thankful. Please remind me to show appreciation for everything the Father has done for me. Give me opportunities to demonstrate my gratefulness for all You have done and continue to do in my life. You have done more than I can ever ask or dream.*

## PRAYER REQUESTS

## PRAISES

## ANSWERS TO PRAYER

# BLESSED PRAYER

Love to pray—feel often during the day the need for prayer, and take trouble to pray. Prayer enlarges the heart until it is capable of containing God's gift of Himself.

MOTHER TERESA

*God, I haven't been very faithful to pray. Forgive me for putting other things before my time with You. You are the most important priority. Without you, I am not. Let my life forever belong to You. Make my heart tender toward time spent with You.*

## PRAISES

## PRAYER REQUESTS

## ANSWERS TO PRAYER

# Day 189
## UNENDING GRACE

The grace you had yesterday will not be sufficient for today.
Grace is the overflowing favor of God, and you can always
count on it being available to draw upon as needed.

OSWALD CHAMBERS

*God, today I ask again for Your grace. I am thankful for Your undeserved,
unearned favor. You bless simply because You love me—not for anything I
have done or could do. Thank You for giving me all the grace I need today.*

## PRAYER REQUESTS

## PRAISES

## ANSWERS TO PRAYER

# Day 190

## GOD GRANTS STRENGTH

But those who hope in the LORD will renew their strength. They will soar on wings like eagles; they will run and not grow weary, they will walk and not be faint.
ISAIAH 40:31 NIV

*God, when I feel like I just can't. . .I know deep down by faith I can. And so for that very reason, I will try. I will put one foot in front of the other, stepping out toward You. Prepare the path You have for me. I listen to Your voice and will continue to follow.*

........................................................................................

........................................................................................

........................................................................................

........................................................................................

........................................................................................

| PRAISES | PRAYER REQUESTS |
|---------|-----------------|
|         |                 |
|         | **ANSWERS TO PRAYER** |
|         |                 |

# Day 191
## ASK FOR WISDOM

Let perseverance finish its work so that you may be mature and complete, not lacking anything. If any of you lacks wisdom, you should ask God, who gives generously to all without finding fault, and it will be given to you. But when you ask, you must believe and not doubt, because the one who doubts is like a wave of the sea, blown and tossed by the wind.
JAMES 1:4–6 NIV

*Today, God, I will persevere! I will not stop. I cannot quit. My heart belongs to You. Thank You for helping me reach full maturity, lacking no good thing. I ask today and receive because I believe You will give me wisdom to succeed.*

PRAYER REQUESTS

PRAISES

ANSWERS TO PRAYER

## Day 192
# THE HOLY SPIRIT

*Lord, one of the greatest gifts You've given me is the Holy Spirit to intercede for me during prayer. Thank You, Holy Spirit, for intervening and making my requests better than I ever could. Holy Spirit, lead me; guide me. Speak to my heart as I pray. Give me the words I need to say so that my prayers are a sweet fragrance to my heavenly Father. Help me to remember the promises of God and stand firm in faith to receive them.*

## PRAISES

## PRAYER REQUESTS

## ANSWERS TO PRAYER

# WONDERFUL ANSWERS

When we hope for an awesome response to our communication with God, it's not because we're so wonderful. Finding the perfect way to ask won't work—that's expecting magic, not faith. But somehow, as we do our ordinary petitioning, God provides the wonderful answers.

*No matter what I ask, God, You have the answer. You know even before I speak what You will say. I come believing in You, asking in faith, and believing I will receive Your answer. It may not be what I expected, but I trust You for what I need.*

## PRAYER REQUESTS

## PRAISES

## ANSWERS TO PRAYER

# Day 194
## FINDING SATISFACTION

Do not spoil what you have by desiring what you have not; but remember
that what you now have was once among the things only hoped for.

EPICURUS

*Lord, I will be content will all You have provided. I settle into a peaceful place,
grateful for Your provision. I remember when what I have today was only a dream.
You make dreams come true. Thank You for putting provision in my hands.*

........................................................................................................................................

........................................................................................................................................

........................................................................................................................................

........................................................................................................................................

........................................................................................................................................

........................................................................................................................................

| PRAISES | PRAYER REQUESTS |
|---|---|
| | |
| | **ANSWERS TO PRAYER** |

# EVER-PRESENT BLESSINGS

When I called upon God to show Himself to me, He blessed me with. . .
a letter bearing good news, a caring voice on the phone, a forgiving heart,
an invitation to share a cup of tea. . .a knock at the door, a new beginning.
God showed Himself through friends, both old and new. I am blessed once more!

UNKNOWN

*God, Your blessings are like raindrops, anticipated and hoped for but always a surprise when they come to my front door. Thank You for the many gifts You've given me. May I forever be grateful for those showers that come. I praise You today as I count each one.*

## PRAYER REQUESTS

## PRAISES

## ANSWERS TO PRAYER

# LIVE GOD'S WAY

But what happens when we live God's way? He brings gifts into
our lives, much the same way that fruit appears in an orchard—
things like affection for others, exuberance about life, serenity.

GALATIANS 5:22 MSG

*God, in my selfishness, I have chosen my own path or tried to make things work out my
own way. I ask for Your forgiveness and receive it today. I repent and turn away from
the desire to have things my own way. Today I look to You and will follow Your plan.*

## PRAISES

## PRAYER REQUESTS

## ANSWERS TO PRAYER

# THANKS AND PRAISE

If anyone would tell you the shortest, surest way to all happiness and all perfection, he must tell you to make it a rule to yourself to thank and praise God for everything that happens to you. For it is certain that whatever seeming calamity happens to you, if you thank and praise God for it, you turn it into a blessing.

WILLIAM LAW

*God, today I thank You for everything You have given me. I even praise You for the difficulties I've had, because each one has given me something good. I learned a lesson or grew closer to You. I found hope again or friendships or strength I never knew I had.*

## PRAYER REQUESTS

## PRAISES

## ANSWERS TO PRAYER

# Day 198
## TRUE HAPPINESS

True happiness comes when we stop complaining about all the troubles
we have and offer thanks for all the troubles we don't have.

*Lord, forgive me when I have complained. I don't want to be the person who sees the glass
half-full. You have filled my cup to overflowing in so many ways. Thank You for the health
I have, the food I eat, the strength I need, and the shelter I call home. I am so blessed.*

## PRAISES

## PRAYER REQUESTS

## ANSWERS TO PRAYER

# Day 199
## GOD'S DELIGHT

I imagine God delights in watching us take on new things, enjoy the world He's created for us, and learn more of Him. He created us because He wanted to share things with us not only in eternity but here on earth too. Scripture contains frequent indications of the joy He has in His creation, and part of that creation is us.

*When new things come my way, I pray I will not shrink from them. Instead help me to embrace each new opportunity to learn, grow, and become more of who You created me to be. Thank You for new ideas and the ability to do something new.*

### PRAYER REQUESTS

### PRAISES

### ANSWERS TO PRAYER

# OPEN DOORS

When one door closes, another one opens, but we often look so long and regretfully at the closed door that we fail to see the one that has opened for us.
ALEXANDER GRAHAM BELL

*Thank You, Lord, for open doors. When a door closes, help me not to grieve what is past but to have an earnest expectation for what is next. May I look eagerly to You for the new opportunities You have for me. Even when it takes a little longer than I'd like, I will not quit. I will wait.*

## PRAISES

## PRAYER REQUESTS

## ANSWERS TO PRAYER

# SMALL JOYS

It isn't the great big pleasures that count the most;
it's making a great deal out of the little ones.
JEAN WEBSTER

~

*Thank You for the small joys—like the smells of yesterday that warm my heart—remembering the precious times with family members. The laughter in Grandma's kitchen, the times of jumping in the leaves with my siblings, and the smell of Daddy's shirt as he held me in his arms.*

........................................................................................................

........................................................................................................

........................................................................................................

........................................................................................................

## PRAYER REQUESTS

........................................................................

........................................................................

........................................................................

........................................................................

## PRAISES

........................................................................

........................................................................

........................................................................

........................................................................

........................................................................

........................................................................

........................................................................

........................................................................

## ANSWERS TO PRAYER

........................................................................

........................................................................

........................................................................

........................................................................

# Day 202
## FIND ACCEPTANCE

Accept the way God does things, for who can straighten what he has
made crooked? Enjoy prosperity while you can, but when hard times strike,
realize that both come from God. Remember that nothing is certain in this life.
ECCLESIASTES 7:13–14 NLT

*Heavenly Father, I am grateful for the twists and turns in life. Though I
didn't expect them and didn't celebrate them at first, I have seen You
take those times and bring about something good. Your ability to help me
overcome anything gives me a willingness to embrace what comes.*

### PRAISES

### PRAYER REQUESTS

### ANSWERS TO PRAYER

## Day 203

# WALK WITH HIM

May your footsteps set you upon a lifetime journey of love.
May you wake each day with His blessings and sleep each night
in His keeping. And may you always walk in His tender care.

*Father, You love me like no one else can. Thank You for loving me uncon-*
*ditionally. There is nothing I can do to take myself out of Your hand. I am*
*thankful for each new day. You are forever watching over me, guiding me*
*tenderly like a parent leads a child, with a gentle hand on my shoulder.*

---

### PRAYER REQUESTS

### PRAISES

### ANSWERS TO PRAYER

*Day 204*

# THE REWARDS OF DILIGENCE

God's best gifts, like valuable jewels, are kept under lock and key, and
those who want them must, with fervent faith, importunately ask for
them; for God is the rewarder of them that diligently seek Him.

D. L. MOODY

*I pause today to thank You for Your best gifts. Your presence is precious
to me. When I seek You, I find You. May I forever remember You will
never let me fail. You reward me with Your presence as I follow hard
after You. Feed my faith, and help me grow in my trust of You.*

### PRAISES

### PRAYER REQUESTS

### ANSWERS TO PRAYER

# NO NEED TO WAIT

If you've been waiting for heaven to enjoy all the joys and delights of faith, turn around. Look at the blessings you've received today, all the things God has done and is doing in your life, and appreciate them. But don't stop there; you can also start taking advantage of the spiritual mission God has given you. Because God never gives us blessings simply to enjoy—every good thing is meant to be shared.

*God, Your blessings are new every morning. Help me to joyfully share those blessings with others. I am grateful for the purpose You've placed in my life. I accept my mission to point others to You and to Your kingdom. Give me opportunities today to share everything good.*

## PRAYER REQUESTS

## PRAISES

## ANSWERS TO PRAYER

## *Day 206*
# LIMITLESS HOPE

When we take time to notice the simple things in life, we never
lack for encouragement. We discover we are surrounded by
limitless hope that's just wearing everyday clothes.

UNKNOWN

*Forgive me, Lord, for seeing the ordinary things in life as mundane and
insignificant. Everything in life You created for my pleasure. I will
open my eyes and ears and tune my senses to experience all the hope
You've placed in and around me. I celebrate YOUR good.*

### PRAISES

### PRAYER REQUESTS

### ANSWERS TO PRAYER

## Day 207

# A SPLENDID GIFT

Live your life while you have it. Life is a
splendid gift—there is nothing small about it.

FLORENCE NIGHTINGALE

*Oh God! Life is a splendid gift. In the past few years I've known too many
who have lost their life here on earth. May I never take a single breath for
granted. I want to cherish the life I have. I am forever grateful to have the
opportunity to live this life with You and those You've given me.*

.......................................................................................................
.......................................................................................................
.......................................................................................................
.......................................................................................................
.......................................................................................................

### PRAYER REQUESTS

.................................................
.................................................
.................................................
.................................................

### ANSWERS TO PRAYER

.................................................
.................................................
.................................................
.................................................

### PRAISES

.................................................
.................................................
.................................................
.................................................
.................................................
.................................................
.................................................
.................................................
.................................................
.................................................
.................................................

# Day 208
## OUR SAFE-COVERING

For the LORD God is a sun and shield; the LORD bestows favor and honor;
no good thing does he withhold from those whose walk is blameless.
PSALM 84:11 NIV

*Lord, I mess up sometimes, and I do want to walk blameless before You.
Help me to stay on the path You've set before me. Forgive me when I
fall; and help me quickly recover and not beat myself up. Thank You for
Your grace, favor, and honor even when I don't think I deserve it.*

### PRAISES

### PRAYER REQUESTS

### ANSWERS TO PRAYER

# Day 209
## BEYOND ALL PROFUSION

I know nothing so pleasant as to sit there on a summer afternoon, with the western sun flickering through the great elder-tree. . .where flowers and flowering shrubs are set as thick as grass in a field, a wilderness blossom, interwoven, intertwined, wreathy, garland, profuse beyond all profusion.

MARY RUSSELL MITFORD

*God, Your creation speaks of Your majesty and the abundance You provide. As I look across this beautiful, lush land, I see Your provision at every turn. All that You created teems with life and was placed here to grow. Thank You for your overwhelming abundance in my life.*

PRAYER REQUESTS

PRAISES

ANSWERS TO PRAYER

## Day 210
# EXCEEDING GREATNESS

*Great beauty, great strength, and great riches are really
and truly of no great use; a right heart exceeds all.*
BENJAMIN FRANKLIN

~~~

*Lord, Your Word says that out of the abundance of the heart, the mouth speaks.
I fill my heart with Your truth. I pour over Your words of scripture and fill my mind with
knowledge and understanding of who You are. May I have a right heart that pleases You.*

.......................................................................................................................................................
.......................................................................................................................................................
.......................................................................................................................................................
.......................................................................................................................................................
.......................................................................................................................................................

### PRAISES

.......................................................
.......................................................
.......................................................
.......................................................
.......................................................
.......................................................
.......................................................
.......................................................
.......................................................

### PRAYER REQUESTS

.......................................................
.......................................................
.......................................................
.......................................................

### ANSWERS TO PRAYER

.......................................................
.......................................................
.......................................................
.......................................................

# KIND WORDS

One of the greatest blessings of the Christian life is a kind word spoken just when you need to hear it. Caring kindness should set Christians apart from unbelievers.

~

*I realize I am not as caring as I should be. Forgive me when I am more focused on myself than the people around me. Please touch my heart and remind me of the mercy and goodness You've shown to me. And because I belong to You, I want to show kindness to others.*

## PRAYER REQUESTS

## PRAISES

## ANSWERS TO PRAYER

# Day 212
## RELISH YOUR HAPPINESS

*Thank You, Lord, for what I do have, which is happiness. Help me be wise with what money I have and use it in a way that pleases You. You love a generous giver, and sometimes I really want to hold on to what I have. My thoughts are toward lack, when Your thoughts are toward plenteousness. I will remember that You are my source. I have everything I need because You are my provider. I will give and trust You for what I need.*

### PRAISES

### PRAYER REQUESTS

### ANSWERS TO PRAYER

# Day 213
## FRESH BLESSINGS

If God grants still to pour fresh blessings upon us, yes, even the greatest of all blessings, salvation, what can we say to these things but, "Thanks be to God for His unspeakable gift!"

*Thank You, God, for saving my soul. I am forever grateful that You put me back together after the fall and made eternal life available to me. It cost You everything; and I sacrificed nothing. Oh, what a gift. May I forever remember all the wonderful things I have because You gave.*

PRAYER REQUESTS

PRAISES

ANSWERS TO PRAYER

# Day 214
## A GENTLE SHEPHERD

The LORD is my shepherd, I will not be in need. He lets me lie down
in green pastures; He leads me beside quiet waters. He restores
my soul; He guides me in the paths of righteousness for the sake of
His name. . . . You prepare a table before me in the presence of my
enemies; You have anointed my head with oil; My cup overflows.

PSALM 23:1–3, 5 NASB

*Lord, I am lost without You. As I look back on the times I've gone ahead
of You, I've made mistakes. You point me toward the road less traveled
and take me on the journey I could never have dreamed. The greatest
adventure requires faith. I trust You, Lord! Help me to believe.*

## PRAISES

## PRAYER REQUESTS

## ANSWERS TO PRAYER

# Day 215

## WE NEED HIM

God does not give us everything we want, but He does fulfill all His
promises. . .leading us along the best and straightest paths to Himself.

DIETRICH BONHOEFFER

*Father, You know what I need before I ask. You know what is good for me
even when I don't. I have lots of questions, and You have all the answers. I am
learning every day that the path You lead me on is the only path for me.*

...........................................................................................................................
...........................................................................................................................
...........................................................................................................................
...........................................................................................................................
...........................................................................................................................
...........................................................................................................................

### PRAYER REQUESTS

...................................................
...................................................
...................................................
...................................................

### PRAISES

...................................................
...................................................
...................................................
...................................................
...................................................
...................................................
...................................................
...................................................
...................................................
...................................................

### ANSWERS TO PRAYER

...................................................
...................................................
...................................................
...................................................

# YOUR SUCCESS

If the day and the night are such that you greet them with joy,
and life emits a fragrance like flowers and sweet-scented herbs,
is more elastic, more starry, more immortal—that is your success.

HENRY DAVID THOREAU

*My success is not determined by what I do each day or what the world
defines as success. I desire to be successful in Your eyes. Full surrender
to Your will is the biggest win. I desire to be everything You see
in me. I want to fulfill Your will in every area of my life.*

## PRAISES

## PRAYER REQUESTS

## ANSWERS TO PRAYER

# Day 217

## NO FLYAWAYS

God doesn't expect His people to trust in flyaway blessings when they can have the very best. He offers Himself as security for this life and eternity. Why would anyone choose anything less?

*God, I don't want any counterfeits in my life. I am grateful for every blessing, but I want to reach my heavenly home and hear You say, "Well done!" I refuse to miss a step. Position me to be in the right place at the right time every time to be a blessing to You.*

........................................................................................................
........................................................................................................
........................................................................................................
........................................................................................................
........................................................................................................
........................................................................................................

### PRAYER REQUESTS

........................................................
........................................................
........................................................
........................................................

### ANSWERS TO PRAYER

........................................................
........................................................
........................................................
........................................................

### PRAISES

........................................................
........................................................
........................................................
........................................................
........................................................
........................................................
........................................................
........................................................
........................................................
........................................................
........................................................
........................................................

# TODAY

Live today! Live fully each moment of today. Trust God to let you work through this moment and the next. He will give you all you need. Don't skip over the painful or confusing moment—even it has its important and rightful place in the day.

⤳

*Sometimes I do want to skip the hard times. But You have given me today, and I will walk through it. Teach me what I need to know in this moment to grow and become all of who You've created me to be. I embrace this moment. Open my eyes to see what You want me to see.*

## PRAISES

## PRAYER REQUESTS

## ANSWERS TO PRAYER

## Day 219

# HAPPY CHARITIES

The happiness of life is made up of minute fractions—
the little, soon-forgotten charities of a kiss or a smile,
a kind look, or heartfelt compliment.

SAMUEL TAYLOR COLERIDGE

*Thank You, Lord, for my family, all of those who bring me joy and show
me affection. I am grateful for every person. Help me to be quick to forgive
and to offer a word of comfort and arms of love. Help me to prefer others.*

## PRAYER REQUESTS

## PRAISES

## ANSWERS TO PRAYER

# READY TO GIVE

"So if you sinful people know how to give good gifts to your children, how much more will your heavenly Father give the Holy Spirit to those who ask him?"
LUKE 11:13 NLT

*Heavenly Father, You are such a good Father. You love me unconditionally. Sometimes I am not ready to receive what You have because I feel unworthy of Your gifts, but You don't think that way. You give good gifts unconditionally. So I open my heart and receive from You today.*

## PRAISES

## PRAYER REQUESTS

## ANSWERS TO PRAYER

# *Day 221*
## THE VERY BEST

Our Creator would never have made such lovely days, and have
given us the deep hearts to enjoy them, above and beyond
all thought, unless we were meant to be immortal.

NATHANIEL HAWTHORNE

*Jesus, thank You for making the sacrifice so that I could spend
eternity with You. Help me to have a long view of life, forever with my
eyes on eternity. Whatever challenges I am facing, it is but for a moment.
The victory has already been won because of what You have done.*

### PRAYER REQUESTS

### PRAISES

### ANSWERS TO PRAYER

# *Day 222*
## ABUNDANT BLESSINGS

However many blessings we expect from God, his infinite
liberality will always exceed all our wishes and our thoughts.
JOHN CALVIN

*God, You are bigger than all my questions; You far exceed my expectations. You know
all my hopes and dreams, and when they line up with Your truth, You make them a
reality. I am grateful for the love You have shown me. No one loves me like You do!*

## PRAISES

## PRAYER REQUESTS

## ANSWERS TO PRAYER

# Day 223

## GOOD INTENTIONS

Abundant life, full of good things on this earth; spiritual peace and joy; and full, satisfying relationships—that's what God intends His people to have. Because Jesus entered your life, you've entered a new realm. Life has taken on a new meaning because you know the Creator.

*Thank You, Father, for new life. I receive Jesus as my Lord and Savior and surrender all to You. I open my heart's door to Jesus and invite Him to create all things new in my life. I will never be the same. Let my life change so much because of You that no one can deny Your intentions for me.*

### PRAYER REQUESTS

### PRAISES

### ANSWERS TO PRAYER

# THREE WELCOMES

May you always find three welcomes in life: in a garden during summer, at a fireside during winter, and whatever the day or season, in the kind eyes of a friend.

*Lord, please help me to welcome others as You have welcomed me. Give me the gift of hospitality. When people are with me, may they experience Your peace. May they feel welcomed, included, and seen not just by me but by You as well.*

## PRAISES

## PRAYER REQUESTS

## ANSWERS TO PRAYER

## Day 225
# SPREAD THE LOVE

Your heart is beating with God's love; open it to others. He has entrusted you with gifts and talents; use them for His service. He goes before you each step of the way; walk in faith. Take courage. Step out into the unknown with the One who knows all.

ELLYN SANNA

*Give me faith and courage today, Lord! May I step out, believing Your love will shine through to others. No matter what others say or think, I will serve You. I will be courageous to do Your will and speak openly about You to others as You lead.*

### PRAYER REQUESTS

### ANSWERS TO PRAYER

### PRAISES

# THE RAINBOW

"I have set my rainbow in the clouds, and it will be the sign of the covenant between me and the earth. Whenever I bring clouds over the earth and the rainbow appears in the clouds, I will remember my covenant between me and you and all living creatures of every kind. Never again will the waters become a flood to destroy all life."

GENESIS 9:13–15 NIV

*Thank You, God, that You are not a human; You cannot lie. You declare a thing, and it becomes reality. You will never let a promise go undelivered. Your Word is always true. You send it forward, and it accomplishes exactly what You said. It will never return to You void. Thank You.*

## PRAISES

## PRAYER REQUESTS

## ANSWERS TO PRAYER

# KEEP WATCH

Be on the lookout for mercies. The more we look for them, the more
of them we will see. Blessings brighten when we count them.

MALTBIE BABCOCK

*Father, Your mercies are new every single morning. No matter how much mercy I may
need, Your supply of mercy never runs out. So today I open my eyes to count the times
You are merciful to me. And each time I will rejoice and sing Your praises. Thank You.*

## PRAYER REQUESTS

## PRAISES

## ANSWERS TO PRAYER

# DAILY JOYS

Daily duties are daily joys, because they are something which God gives us to offer unto Him, to do to our very best, in acknowledgment of His love.

EDWARD BOUVERIE PUSEY

*I am grateful for the little messes that spring up every single day. Each one is a reminder that I have people I love, an abundant supply of blessings, and every need met. Forgive me when I grumble, and remind me to celebrate instead of complain. Thank You for the opportunity to do it all for You.*

## PRAISES

## PRAYER REQUESTS

## ANSWERS TO PRAYER

## Day 229

# THE GREAT PROVIDER

Whether we are joyful or sad, God still remains faithful. He provides our needs even if we don't get the lavish things we'd prefer. And He always provides generous spiritual blessings for those who trust in Him. No matter what your circumstances, you can always cling to Jesus—and be blessed.

*You are forever faithful. No matter what comes—opposition, discouragement, grief, or disappointment—You forever remain by my side. You build me up with Your Word. You make a way when I see no way. You are the hope I hold on to through the tough times.*

### PRAYER REQUESTS

### PRAISES

### ANSWERS TO PRAYER

# Day 230
## WORK = GRACE

Our work is meant to be a grace. It is a blessing and a gift, even a surprise
and an act of unconditional love, toward the community—and not just
the present community that may or may not compensate us for our work,
but the community to come, the generations that follow our work.

MATTHEW FOX

*Lord, help me to be an example to the next generation. May I be remembered for my faith
and unconditional love expressed not just to those who are easy to love but also to those
who are more difficult. Give me peace and strength to have a reputation that honors You.*

PRAISES

PRAYER REQUESTS

ANSWERS TO PRAYER

# *Day 231*

# SO SMALL A THING

It is so small a thing to have enjoyed the sun, to have lived light in the spring,
to have loved, to have thought, to have done; to have advanced true friends.

M. ARNOLD

*I take great joy each day in every little thing You have given.*
*Remind me to look up and see all the things You've provided around me.*
*I celebrate the little things today. Remind me to love extravagantly.*

.................................................................................................................
.................................................................................................................
.................................................................................................................
.................................................................................................................
.................................................................................................................
.................................................................................................................

## PRAYER REQUESTS

## PRAISES

## ANSWERS TO PRAYER

# Day 232
## CELEBRATE!

"You will go out in joy and be led forth in peace; the mountains and hills will burst into song before you, and all the trees of the field will clap their hands. Instead of the thornbush will grow the juniper, and instead of briers the myrtle will grow."

ISAIAH 55:12–13 NIV

*Jesus, You can soften the hard things in life through the comfort You provide to my soul. I can't imagine doing life without You. You bring me out of the darkness and shine Your light into my soul. Only then can I truly see the truth of who I am in You.*

## PRAISES

## PRAYER REQUESTS

## ANSWERS TO PRAYER

# Day 233
## AS BIG AS LIFE

Life without hope is an empty, boring, and useless life. I cannot imagine that I could strive for something if I did not carry hope in me. I am thankful to God for this gift. It is as big as life itself.

VÁCLAV HAVEL

*Holy Spirit, You are the hope of Christ in me. Each day I live to give that hope to others. Show me how to fill my soul with hope each day so that I am full to overflowing. That way I can pour hope into the lives of others who need to experience Christ.*

PRAYER REQUESTS

PRAISES

ANSWERS TO PRAYER

# HIS KISS OF PEACE

May God kiss you with His peace as a father kisses his little
child. And may you know that peace isn't a pot of gold rewarded
to you after chasing some rainbow's end—it's a gift.

*Heavenly Father, I receive Your peace. It is a sweet and precious gift given freely with
no strings attached. I've done nothing to deserve it, and yet it is mine as sure as my
salvation. I am grateful to live each day embraced by You. I have no reason to fear.*

## PRAISES

## PRAYER REQUESTS

## ANSWERS TO PRAYER

## Day 235

# ALWAYS IN BLOOM

No matter what season of life you're in, you should bloom. Ask God to help you
do the best you can. Ask Him to help you be a blessing wherever you are.

*God, I am blessed to be a blessing. Let my roots dig deep into relationship*
*with You so that I grow in a way that pleases You. May I truly live*
*an authentic life in You. May others see the real reason I bloom with*
*blessings from heaven. Help me to be a blessing everywhere I go.*

---

### PRAYER REQUESTS

### PRAISES

### ANSWERS TO PRAYER

# Day 236
## UNSUNG HEROES

The lives that have been the greatest blessing to you are the lives of those
people who themselves were unaware of having been a blessing.

OSWALD CHAMBERS

*Lord, I am not always good at letting people know what a blessing they are
in my life. I want to take the time to show them in meaningful ways what
a gift they are. Show me how to let them know this. Give me Your words
to share with them and thoughtful ideas of how I can bless them.*

........................................................................................................

........................................................................................................

........................................................................................................

........................................................................................................

........................................................................................................

### PRAISES

### PRAYER REQUESTS

### ANSWERS TO PRAYER

# GIVE AS ANGELS GIVE

Instead of a gem, or even a flower, we should cast the gift of a loving
thought into the heart of a friend, that would be giving as the angels give.
GEORGE MACDONALD

*Lord, I want to add to the lives of others, not take away. Help me stay positive and
joyful no matter what life brings. I choose to have a grateful attitude. May I always
think good thoughts about other people and express them when I have the opportunity.*

## PRAYER REQUESTS

## PRAISES

## ANSWERS TO PRAYER

# Day 238
## A SPECIAL GIFT

Christ gave each one of us the special gift of grace, showing how generous he is. That is why it says in the Scriptures, "When he went up to the heights, he led a parade of captives, and he gave gifts to people."

EPHESIANS 4:7–8 NCV

*Jesus, I tap into Your gift of grace. I don't want to jump to conclusions when things go south. Help me to keep an open mind and carefully evaluate each situation before I respond. I invite You to participate in all my conversations. I choose to give gifts of grace to others today.*

## PRAISES

## PRAYER REQUESTS

## ANSWERS TO PRAYER

# *Day 239*
## SHARING HEARTS

Over cups of tea, I listened to my friend, and my friend heard me.
My joy was hers and hers was mine, as we shared our hearts line by line.
UNKNOWN

*Lord, thank You for my precious friends. I am grateful for those who
I may not see for a long season and yet we can pick up just where we
left off. I so appreciate the way our hearts are intertwined. We are not
just friends but family. May each one see the gift they are to me.*

PRAYER REQUESTS

PRAISES

ANSWERS TO PRAYER

# Day 240

## UNDERESTIMATED

The sun. . .in its full glory, either at the rising or setting. . .this, and many
other like blessings, we enjoy daily. And for most of them, because they
be so common, most men forget to pay their praises: but let not us.

IZAAK WALTON

*I sing Your praise today, my Creator. I rejoice at the sights I see. Each one is a reminder of
the care You take of me. You created each part of my world for me to enjoy and to provide
for me. I don't want to take a single thing for granted. For each one, I sing Your praises.*

PRAISES

PRAYER REQUESTS

ANSWERS TO PRAYER

## Day 241

# RIGHT NOW

You don't have to be facing the end of your life to be blessed by Jesus.
He wants to bless you today. He wants to shower many blessings on
you for a lifetime instead of limiting His impact to a few years.

*Jesus, because I have given my life to You, I have the promise of eternity. May I never
forget that this life is but a flicker of the life I have to live. The things that seem so big
to me today are nothing in comparison to the life I have to live. My eternity is now.*

### PRAYER REQUESTS

### PRAISES

### ANSWERS TO PRAYER

# Day 242
## PASS IT ON

Have you had a kindness shown? Pass it on; 'twas not given for thee alone, pass it on; let it travel down the years, let it wipe another's tears, till in heaven the deed appears, pass it on.
HENRY BURTON

*Thank You for the little kindnesses I've been given. It is Your favor on my life that causes others to notice and bless me. Help me to live each day with a hope of passing kindness—Your kindness—to others. Don't let me talk myself out of it, but when the thought comes, I will act.*

### PRAISES

### PRAYER REQUESTS

### ANSWERS TO PRAYER

## Day 243
# A NEVER-ENDING LIST

*Heavenly Father, I have so much to be thankful for. My list of blessings is never ending. May I never fail to praise You and to thank You for the many blessings You have given to me. Thank You for the people I love and those who love me. Thank You for each favor and kind word others show me. Thank You for providing for my household and giving me the opportunity to share with others. When I think about each blessing, I will praise You.*

## PRAYER REQUESTS

## ANSWERS TO PRAYER

## PRAISES

# Day 244
## SHINE

"You are the light that gives light to the world. A city that is built on a hill cannot be hidden. And people don't hide a light under a bowl. They put it on a lampstand so the light shines for all the people in the house. In the same way, you should be a light for other people. Live so that they will see the good things you do and will praise your Father in heaven."

MATTHEW 5:14–16 NCV

*Jesus, even on the hard days, when I want to seclude myself from the world, I will respond to Your love and step outside to shine Your light so that others may experience You. Give me strength to be the light You have asked me to be.*

---

### PRAISES

### PRAYER REQUESTS

### ANSWERS TO PRAYER

# REST IN HIM

When God finds a soul that rests in Him and is not easily moved. . .He gives to such a soul the key to the treasures He has prepared for it so that it might enjoy them.

CATHERINE OF GENOA

*God, help me to be that soul that rests in You and is not easily moved. I want to trust You with an unbreakable bond. I want to believe, especially when I don't see it yet. Thank You for preparing me for what is to come. I accept each treasure by faith.*

## PRAYER REQUESTS

## PRAISES

## ANSWERS TO PRAYER

# GOD-GIVEN PURPOSE

You are here in order to enable the world to live more amply, with greater vision, with a finer spirit of hope and achievement. You are here to enrich the world, and you impoverish yourself if you forget the errand.

WOODROW WILSON

*Lord, You said I am the light of the world, set on a hill for everyone to see. I don't always feel like a light or even really want to be one, but I know You have given me that purpose. So, I accept that gift and will rise to the challenge to become who You've created me to be.*

## PRAISES

## PRAYER REQUESTS

## ANSWERS TO PRAYER

# Day 247
## GOD'S BEST GIFT

No matter what gifts God gives us, we are to receive them with thanks. He made these gifts just for us, and we're enjoying the benefit, so why not share that joy with Jesus? He's the best gift God had to offer, the gift most to be received with thanksgiving.

*Jesus, You are the most perfect gift ever given. I receive You and believe You. Thank You for enduring the cross, making the exchange of my sin for Your sinlessness, my death for Your life. I am grateful for Your willingness to do the will of the Father. I follow Your example.*

### PRAYER REQUESTS

### PRAISES

### ANSWERS TO PRAYER

## Day 248
# THE GOLDEN LINK

A mother's love is indeed the golden link that binds youth to age; and he
is still but a child. . .who can yet recall, with a softened heart, the fond
devotion, or the gentle chidings, of the best friend that God ever gives us.
CHRISTIAN NESTELL BOVEE

*Thank You for my mother, Lord. Show me how to honor her in a way
that pleases You. Let the words of my mouth bless her and my thoughts
toward her tend to blessing. Give her strength to live all the days You've set
before her that she may know You and enjoy the blessings of family.*

### PRAISES

### PRAYER REQUESTS

### ANSWERS TO PRAYER

# Day 249

## GOD IS EVERYWHERE

There's not a tint that paints the rose, or decks the lily fair,
Or streaks the humblest flower that grows, but God has placed it there. . . .
There's not a place on earth's vast round, in ocean's deep or air,
Where skill and wisdom are not found, for God is everywhere.

JAMES C. WALLACE

*God, thank You for who You are. Whether I go up or down, across or beneath, Your beautiful presence greets me. You knew me from the inside out even before I was born, and I am so thankful to have a relationship with someone who knows me so well and loves me.*

### PRAYER REQUESTS

### PRAISES

### ANSWERS TO PRAYER

# Day 250
## DELIGHTFUL BLESSINGS

Take delight in the LORD, and he will give you the desires of your heart. Commit your way to the LORD; trust in him and he will do this: he will make your righteous reward shine like the dawn, your vindication like the noonday sun.

PSALM 37:4–6 NIV

*Lord, sometimes I'm deceived in thinking my own way is right. When all the curtains of doubt and deception are pulled away, I can see clearly that You have the very best plans for me. Help me to surrender fully to Your will and submit to Your plan. Only then will I experience true delight.*

## PRAISES

## PRAYER REQUESTS

## ANSWERS TO PRAYER

# Day 251
## CONFIDENCE REGAINED

*Lord, help me to get over this nagging self-doubt. Remind me that Your bless-
ings are forever and I have nothing to fear. Give me a merry heart, I pray. You
have given me everything I need to succeed. Worry does nothing but suck the life
out of me. I am victorious always when I stand in faith, trusting and believing
in You. I cannot fail as long as I am in You. I can because You already did.*

---

### PRAYER REQUESTS

### PRAISES

### ANSWERS TO PRAYER

## *Day 252*
# THE KEY TO RENEWAL

By reading the scriptures I am so renewed that all nature seems
renewed around me and with me. The sky seems to be a pure,
a cooler blue, the trees a deeper green. The whole world is charged
with the glory of God, and I feel fire and music under my feet.

THOMAS MERTON

*You make all things new. Your Word is truth. It is food to my soul. I gain nourishment
from it for my soul just as if I were eating physical food for my body. New life comes
from what I embrace. Your Word strengthens me, refreshes me, and renews me.*

### PRAISES

### PRAYER REQUESTS

### ANSWERS TO PRAYER

# GOD'S SPECIAL OFFER

This bright new day, complete with 24 hours of opportunities, choices, and attitudes, comes with a perfectly matched set of 1,440 minutes. This unique gift, this one day, cannot be exchanged, replaced, or refunded. Handle with care. Make the most of it. There is only one per customer!

*Lord, thank You for today. It is a day You created for me to enjoy my life with You. I don't want to squander it by being selfish or putting myself first. Help me to use every minute to share Your truth with others and grow in my own faith. I rejoice while the day is still today.*

........................................................................................................................................

........................................................................................................................................

........................................................................................................................................

........................................................................................................................................

........................................................................................................................................

## PRAYER REQUESTS

........................................................................

........................................................................

........................................................................

........................................................................

## PRAISES

........................................................................

........................................................................

........................................................................

........................................................................

........................................................................

........................................................................

........................................................................

........................................................................

........................................................................

........................................................................

## ANSWERS TO PRAYER

........................................................................

........................................................................

........................................................................

........................................................................

# WELLSPRING OF JOY

*Father, when happiness is hard to come by, help me to learn to draw more consistently on Your wellspring of joy. Help me delight in the little gifts You bring my way every day. Father, Jesus said we would endure hardship, trials, and disappointment. He was rejected, persecuted, and killed because of who He was. When I am struggling because this world is not my home, may I remain joyful and thankful for all that Jesus went through for me.*

## PRAISES

## PRAYER REQUESTS

## ANSWERS TO PRAYER

# BIBLICAL BLESSINGS

The Bible is one of the greatest blessings bestowed by God on the children
of men. . . . It is all pure, all sincere; nothing too much; nothing wanting.

JOHN LOCKE

*Thank You, God, for the Bible. Your Holy Word is life to me. May it always be in my
heart and mind and springing from my lips. It brings the promise yet to be fulfilled of Your
blessings in my life and hope that I will accomplish what You put me on this earth to do.*

## PRAYER REQUESTS

## PRAISES

## ANSWERS TO PRAYER

# Day 256

## SAVING LOVE

"The LORD your God is with you, the Mighty Warrior who saves.
He will take great delight in you; in his love he will no longer
rebuke you, but will rejoice over you with singing."

ZEPHANIAH 3:17 NIV

*Wow! You dance over me with singing. What an awesome word picture of Your great love.
You delight in me even when I can't delight in myself. You love me unconditionally, and
for that I am grateful. Thank You for saving me from everything I need to be saved from.*

......................................................................................................

......................................................................................................

......................................................................................................

......................................................................................................

......................................................................................................

### PRAISES

### PRAYER REQUESTS

### ANSWERS TO PRAYER

# Day 257

## GRATITUDE

Gratitude consists in a watchful, minute attention to the particulars of our state, and to the multitude of God's gifts, taken one by one. It fills us with a consciousness that God loves and cares for us, even to the least event and smallest need of life.

HENRY EDWARD MANNING

*God, I cherish Your gifts in my life. Remind me to take out and carefully examine the treasures You've given me like I would a gift from someone very dear to me. Your sacrifice was tremendous in order to restore me to You. Thank You for believing I would choose You.*

### PRAYER REQUESTS

### PRAISES

### ANSWERS TO PRAYER

# CHANNELS FOR SHARING

God has given us two hands—one to receive with and the other to give with.
We are not cisterns made for hoarding; we are channels made for sharing.

BILLY GRAHAM

*In Acts, the church shared everything so that no one went without.*
*Forgive us, Lord, for hoarding and keeping things for ourselves.*
*Help me to approach those You ask me to bless without judgment or*
*criticism. You gave with arms wide open. Help me to do the same.*

## PRAISES

## PRAYER REQUESTS

## ANSWERS TO PRAYER

## Day 259
# PERFECT TIMING

He made the moon to mark the seasons, and the sun knows when to go
down. . . . Then people go out to their work, to their labor until evening.
How many are your works, Lord! In wisdom you made them all.
PSALM 104:19, 23–24 NIV

*Lord, You know exactly what I'm waiting for. Waiting is so hard, but I trust You. You are
at work behind the scenes even though I can't see it. I trust You are working all things to
my good just as You have promised. I will trust Your timing to be perfect. It always is.*

## PRAYER REQUESTS

## PRAISES

## ANSWERS TO PRAYER

## Day 260
# BE GLAD

Be glad that your life has been full and complete,
Be glad that you've tasted the bitter and sweet. . . .
Be glad that you've had such a full, happy life,
Be glad for your joy as well as your strife. . . .
Be glad for the comfort that you've found in prayer.
Be glad for God's blessings, His love, and His care.

HELEN STEINER RICE

*Without You, Lord, I would be lost. My life is full because You gave me life.
You took my broken heart and created it anew. I am not the same person I was
before I found You. Each day is a gift. I celebrate the life I have in You.*

## PRAISES

## PRAYER REQUESTS

## ANSWERS TO PRAYER

# Day 261

## LOVE LETTERS

The Bible is God's love letter to you. It isn't the sappy romance novel found in drugstores. . . He is communicating His love to you. It's the love letter you've longed to read. Open it and see for yourself.

*Lord, thank You for seeing me! You gave me Your Word that I might know You personally. I am grateful for the way You speak to me as I experience Your Word. Your love pours out over me with each new understanding of who You are.*

### PRAYER REQUESTS

### PRAISES

### ANSWERS TO PRAYER

# Day 262
## BLESSED REWARDS

"Blessed are the merciful, for they shall receive mercy. Blessed are the pure in heart, for they shall see God. Blessed are the peacemakers, for they shall be called sons of God. Blessed are those who are persecuted for righteousness' sake, for theirs is the kingdom of heaven."

MATTHEW 5:7–10 ESV

*Jesus, teach me to be like You. Help me to show mercy just as I have received it from the Father. Cleanse my heart, and show me how to be a peacemaker. I want to experience every gift Your sacrifice provided. I embrace Your gift of salvation.*

### PRAISES

### PRAYER REQUESTS

### ANSWERS TO PRAYER

*Day 263*

# THE KINGDOM ON EARTH

The kingdom of heaven and the kingdom of God are two
phrases for the same thing. They mean not merely a future
happy state in heaven but a state to be enjoyed on earth.
JOHN WESLEY

*Thank You, God, for eternal life. I am living each day with You now. I don't
have to wait for eternity to come, but I embrace the present. May I experience heaven on earth as I walk with You on my journey called today.*

.................................................................................................................
.................................................................................................................
.................................................................................................................
.................................................................................................................
.................................................................................................................

## PRAYER REQUESTS

.....................................................
.....................................................
.....................................................
.....................................................

## PRAISES

.....................................................
.....................................................
.....................................................
.....................................................
.....................................................
.....................................................
.....................................................
.....................................................
.....................................................
.....................................................
.....................................................

## ANSWERS TO PRAYER

.....................................................
.....................................................
.....................................................
.....................................................

# DAILY REFLECTION

The wonderful thing about sunset, and much the same can be said for sunrise, is that it happens every day, and even if the sunset itself is not spectacular, it marks the beginning of the end of another day. It's a great time to pause and take notice.

ELAINE ST. JAMES

*Father, it seems at times life is spinning, and I have no control over how quickly the days pass. I look up and another day, week, or month has gone by. Help me to pause frequently each day to take in the moments You've given me. Remind me to stop and celebrate You.*

.............................................................................................................................

.............................................................................................................................

.............................................................................................................................

.............................................................................................................................

.............................................................................................................................

## PRAISES

## PRAYER REQUESTS

## ANSWERS TO PRAYER

# Day 265

## OVERWHELMING GRACE

Grace is such an overwhelming blessing that most of us dance around
our understanding of it. We have a hard time understanding the
completeness of it, the purity of it, the overwhelming comfort it offers.
But, oh Father, this is a gift, a promise like no other. It sets us free.

*Father, thank You for Your unconditional love. Because You love me, You've given me
unmerited favor and overflowing blessings—not as a result of anything I have done or
could ever do but simply because of who You are. Show me how to give grace to others too.*

PRAYER REQUESTS

PRAISES

ANSWERS TO PRAYER

# Day 266

## PRECIOUS MOMENTS

*Dear Lord, thank You for life's milestones that give us the opportunity to reflect on the bountiful gifts You've bestowed on us. May Your continued blessings be upon us as we celebrate each birthday, wedding, and funeral, always mindful of how precious each and every moment of our lives is. It's easy to forget to celebrate the little things, but it's all the little things that add up that make the life You've given me so powerful and precious. Thank You for all the memories that remind me how You've been at work in my life. I cherish the times You've given me.*

---

### PRAISES

### PRAYER REQUESTS

### ANSWERS TO PRAYER

## Day 267
# FAITH

Faith is the virtue by which, clinging to the faithfulness of God,
we lean upon Him so that we may obtain what he gives us.
WILLIAM AMES

*Oh God! You are forever faithful. Nothing can keep me from Your presence. No one can remove me from Your hand. I hold tight to Your promises that can never be broken. Your Word stands firm! I press into You. I will receive everything I need from You in Your time.*

........................................................................................................

........................................................................................................

........................................................................................................

........................................................................................................

........................................................................................................

........................................................................................................

### PRAYER REQUESTS

........................................................

........................................................

........................................................

........................................................

### PRAISES

........................................

........................................

........................................

........................................

........................................

........................................

........................................

........................................

........................................

........................................

........................................

### ANSWERS TO PRAYER

........................................................

........................................................

........................................................

........................................................

## Day 268

# HIS MASTERPIECE

We are God's masterpiece. He has created us anew in Christ Jesus,
so we can do the good things he planned for us long ago.

EPHESIANS 2:10 NLT

*Sometimes I don't feel like I am fearfully and wonderfully made. Help me to stand my ground, believing all that Your Word says about me. I stand in the authority You've given me to silence the whispers of the enemy. I fill my heart with who You say I am in Christ.*

### PRAISES

### PRAYER REQUESTS

### ANSWERS TO PRAYER

# Day 269
## FATHER KNOWS BEST

*It's a hard truth to swallow, but You know what is best for us, and sometimes Your answer to a prayer is no. Lord, thank You for having the wisdom to know when to tell me no. Father, I trust You. Forgive me for when I struggle to fix things myself or try to control something going on in my life. Teach me to approach life with palms open and face up. Everything in my life is Yours. I surrender all to You so that I can experience all You have for me.*

PRAYER REQUESTS

PRAISES

ANSWERS TO PRAYER

## Day 270
# BLESSINGS IN EVERYTHING

Blessings come in many guises, That God alone in love devises,
And sickness, which we dread so much, Can bring a very healing touch. . . .
And through long hours of tribulation, God gives us time for meditation,
And no sickness can be counted loss that teaches us to bear our cross.

HELEN STEINER RICE

*God, You give good gifts! Even when I face challenges in life that are painful,
You use them for my good. I embrace whatever it is I need to know or
learn through the trials I face. Nothing I go through is wasted. You walk
with me and bring about good from every negative situation.*

### PRAISES

### PRAYER REQUESTS

### ANSWERS TO PRAYER

## Day 271

# MEMORABLE FOOTPRINTS

Life is full of people who will make you laugh, cry, smile until your face hurts, and so happy that you think you'll burst. But the ones who leave their footprints on your soul are the ones that keep your life going.

NATALIE BERNOT

*Thank You for the journey, Lord, with those You bring into my life. I am grateful for the lessons each one has given me, the encouragement when I needed it, and even the hardship that You've brought me through. I celebrate those precious friendships.*

## PRAYER REQUESTS

## PRAISES

## ANSWERS TO PRAYER

# EAGER ANTICIPATION

On that day when every tongue confesses that Jesus is Lord, we will experience the purest pleasure. Giving Jesus the glory on that day will be our greatest delight— one we look forward to with anticipation even now. We yearn for that glorious day.

*What a day it will be! Lord Jesus, I am eagerly anticipating the day when You return for me. This life I live now is far from anything I could imagine that I will experience in the days in heaven with You. Thank You for the hope of forever spent with You.*

## PRAISES

## PRAYER REQUESTS

## ANSWERS TO PRAYER

# OPPORTUNITIES EVERYWHERE

Embrace the wonder and excitement each day brings.
For tomorrow affords us new opportunities. . .time to
experience. . .time to create. . .time to reflect. . .time to dream.

K. WILLIAMS

*I wake each morning with excitement for what the day holds. I have learned to look for the splendor of heaven in the moment. I embrace the surprises You've created for me today. I will pause throughout my day to stop and celebrate the opportunities You set in place.*

## PRAYER REQUESTS

## PRAISES

## ANSWERS TO PRAYER

# ABUNDANT SHOWERS

Rejoice in the LORD your God, for he has given you the autumn
rains because he is faithful. He sends you abundant showers,
both autumn and spring rains, as before. The threshing floors will
be filled with grain; the vats will overflow with new wine and oil.

JOEL 2:23–24 NIV

*God, You have sustained me in the tough times. You have provided for me and made
me flourish in the desert. You have shined Your light into the nighttimes of my life and
brought me into a place of abundance. You are my source. I depend on no one but You.*

## PRAISES

## PRAYER REQUESTS

## ANSWERS TO PRAYER

# Day 275

## PRAISE HIM!

For the invasion of my soul by Thy Holy Spirit: for all human love
and goodness that speaks to me of Thee: for the fullness of Thy
glory outpoured in Jesus Christ: I give Thee thanks, O God.

JOHN BAILLIE

*Holy Spirit, You are welcome in this place. Fill my soul to overflowing with the goodness of God. Show me how to love in a way that brings glory to the Father in heaven. Love through me. Speak to me and show me His great love so that I may share it with others.*

PRAYER REQUESTS

PRAISES

ANSWERS TO PRAYER

# Day 276

## UNCHANGEABLE BEAUTY

The beauty of the earth, the beauty of the sky, the order of the stars, the sun, the moon. . .their very loveliness is their confession of God: For who made these lovely mutable things, but He who is Himself unchangeable beauty?

AUGUSTINE OF HIPPO

*God, thank You for being the one who never changes. I can depend on You to remain the same from age to age. May I grow in my relationship with You so that I know You even more and experience Your splendor and majesty.*

### PRAISES

### PRAYER REQUESTS

### ANSWERS TO PRAYER

# Day 277

## OUR PERSONAL STOREHOUSE

Memories are very private things, a personal storehouse of treasures and sorrows. What a gift God gave us when He created our brains with the ability to remember!

*God, I so appreciate the gift of memory. I don't take it for granted. I love being able to recall the special moments with my family, the memorable stories that stir my heart. As I count my blessings, I am so thankful for each challenge in life You've brought me through.*

### PRAYER REQUESTS

### PRAISES

### ANSWERS TO PRAYER

## Day 278
# GO WITH PURPOSE

We may run, walk, stumble. . .or fly, but let us never lose sight of the
reason for the journey or miss a chance to see a rainbow on the way.
GLORIA GAITHER

*Father, I believe I was born for such a time as this. You knew me before I was ever
born, and You set me on a course of success as I choose to obey You. It is success
defined by heaven, not by those in this world. And in all I do, I want to please You.*

### PRAISES

### PRAYER REQUESTS

### ANSWERS TO PRAYER

## Day 279
# OUR FRIEND, JESUS

The Creator thinks enough of you to have sent Someone very special so that you might have life—abundantly, joyfully, completely, and victoriously.

~⁓

*Jesus is the reason I live. Thank You, Father, for sending Him to knock on my heart's door and for softening my heart enough to have wisdom to receive Him. I am assured of a victorious life in Christ. Thank You for my friend and advocate, Jesus.*

PRAYER REQUESTS

PRAISES

ANSWERS TO PRAYER

# HE IS WAITING

Yet the LORD longs to be gracious to you; therefore he will rise up to show you compassion. For the LORD is a God of justice. Blessed are all who wait for him!
ISAIAH 30:18 NIV

*Father, thank You for the compassion You have shown me. For those who have done injustice to me, it doesn't always feel like they get what they deserve, but You didn't give me what I deserved either. Help me be more compassionate to others just as You have been to me.*

## PRAISES

## PRAYER REQUESTS

## ANSWERS TO PRAYER

## Day 281
# DON'T DESPAIR!

Refuse to be discouraged, refuse to be distressed,
For when we are despondent, our lives cannot be blessed.
For doubt and fear and worry close the door to faith and prayer,
And there's no room for blessings when we're lost in deep despair. . . .
But when we view our problems through the eyes of God above,
Misfortunes turn to blessings and hatred turns to love.

HELEN STEINER RICE

*I encourage myself in You, my Lord! I will not be stressed out. I take You at Your word and will not fear. Anxiety and worry do not belong to me. Instead I will stand strong in faith, believing You will do all You have promised. Thank You for delivering me.*

## PRAYER REQUESTS

## PRAISES

## ANSWERS TO PRAYER

# *Day 282*
## LIVING FOR CHRIST

Living for Christ through His Spirit offers real life, overflowing and abundant.
Blessings spill over in obedient lives. . . . Put to death worldly misdeeds,
and instead of the emptiness of the world, you'll receive blessings indeed!

*I choose each day to live for You. Forever I belong to You. You are my hope and the
lifter of my head. I look to You for my every need. The world and what it offers does not
interest me. You are my source. All I have and all I ever need come from Your hand.*

### PRAISES

### PRAYER REQUESTS

### ANSWERS TO PRAYER

# RECOGNITION

God recognizes that we have received His forgiveness through His Son, and He's happy to grant us our wishes. He gives good things that make us happy. That doesn't mean He gives us everything we ask for. But when we ask in Jesus' will, God is happy to give.

*God, You are a good Father. Thank You for giving to me. You have given me abundant life and filled my soul with every eternal blessing. I am forever grateful for the blessings You have poured out in this life as well. Thank You for providing what is best for me.*

## PRAYER REQUESTS

## PRAISES

## ANSWERS TO PRAYER

## Day 284
# HE WILL PROVIDE

God wants nothing from us except our needs, and these furnish Him with
room to display His bounty when He supplies them freely. . . . Not what I have,
but what I do not have, is the first point of contact between my soul and God.

CHARLES SPURGEON

*Today I bring my needs before You. You know exactly what I have need*
*of even before I ask, but I ask today in faith. And Lord, if it be Your*
*will, then I trust that You will not withhold any good thing from me.*
*I await with earnest expectation to do what You desire in my life.*

## PRAISES

## PRAYER REQUESTS

## ANSWERS TO PRAYER

# STRONG FRIENDSHIPS

Life is a chronicle of friendship. Friends create a world anew each day. Without their loving care, courage would not suffice to keep hearts strong for life.

HELEN KELLER

*Thank You for the strong friendships You have given me. Lord, I pray for each one You bring before me today. I trust You are working in their lives to bring blessing to them. I appreciate each one and the special gifts they bring to my life. Fill them with Your love.*

## PRAYER REQUESTS

## PRAISES

## ANSWERS TO PRAYER

# Day 286
## PEACEFUL SLEEP

It is vain for you to rise up early, to sit up late, to eat the
bread of sorrows; for so He gives His beloved sleep.

PSALM 127:2 NKJV

*You have promised me sweet sleep. Sometimes I struggle to receive it. I let my mind
wonder about things I should not. I turn my thoughts to Your Word. I meditate on
scripture. I receive Your peace and comfort and thank You for restful, deep sleep.*

## PRAISES

## PRAYER REQUESTS

## ANSWERS TO PRAYER

## *Day 287*
# MORNING PRAYER

*Dear Lord, thank You for another new day. Help me taste the richness of the coffee in my cup, and prepare me to recognize Your bountiful blessings in unexpected places. Remind me not to take these tiny treasures for granted. Give me a child's heart that sees the lovely, simple things in life. I don't know why we seem to lose our high hopes and dreams as we get older. Lord, renew my childlikeness. Help me to become more like a wide-eyed child, expecting Your promises to be more than I can ever dream. I want to dream again and believe those dreams will come true.*

## PRAYER REQUESTS

## PRAISES

## ANSWERS TO PRAYER

# SWEET SURPRISES

Into our lives come many things to break the dull routine—
The things we had not planned on that happen unforeseen:
The unexpected little joys that are scattered on our way,
Success we did not count on or a rare, fulfilling day. . . .
And every happening and every lucky break
Are little gifts from God above that are ours to freely take.

HELEN STEINER RICE

*Thank You, Lord, for the unexpected. I appreciate the belly laughs,*
*the genuine surprises, and the rare and unforeseen good things*
*You bring into my life. Instead of being upset because my schedule was*
*interrupted, may I embrace it and celebrate it with thanksgiving to You.*

## PRAISES

## PRAYER REQUESTS

## ANSWERS TO PRAYER

## Day 289
# UNEXPECTED GIFTS

A much-needed gift received at the perfect moment is always welcome even if it comes at no special holiday. God knows that—and understands the importance of timing for everything He gives. . . His presents are always timely, are always perfect, and are certain to be received with thanks by a heart that's truly His.

*God, You lift my heart when I feel low. You know what my soul needs and provide a gift to soothe it at just the right time. Thank You for Your good and perfect gifts in my life. I belong to You. My heart is Yours. I am forever grateful for Your generosity toward me.*

## PRAYER REQUESTS

## PRAISES

## ANSWERS TO PRAYER

# Day 290
## NATURE'S TREASURES

If we are children of God, we have a tremendous treasure in nature and will realize that it is holy and sacred. We will see God reaching out to us in every wind that blows, every sunrise and sunset, every cloud in the sky, every flower that blooms, and every leaf that fades.

OSWALD CHAMBERS

*Thank You, God, for looking down from heaven for me. I seek You and desire to understand You. Everywhere I look, I see You reaching for me, desiring to have relationship with me. I am grateful for Your love and compassion on me.*

PRAISES

PRAYER REQUESTS

ANSWERS TO PRAYER

# *Day 291*
## DAILY NOURISHMENT

Family life is full of major and minor crises—the ups and downs of health, success and failure in careers, marriage, and divorce—and all kinds of characters. . . . With all of these felt details, life etches itself into memory and personality. It's difficult to imagine anything more nourishing to the soul.

THOMAS MOORE

*Thank You, Father, for family—both those born into it and those who have been invited to become my family. Give us peace and patience to love one another through the ups and downs. Help us to stop and care for one another, making special memories that include You.*

### PRAYER REQUESTS

### PRAISES

### ANSWERS TO PRAYER

# Day 292
## LAVISH BLESSINGS

How great is the goodness you have stored up for those who fear you. You lavish it on those who come to you for protection, blessing them before the watching world.

PSALM 31:19 NLT

*Lord, thank You for Your mercy and protection. I appreciate the way You hide me in the shelter of Your wings, like an eagle protects her young. You spread Your feathers over me and keep me safe. Thank You for making sure I am always safe in the right place at the right time.*

### PRAISES

### PRAYER REQUESTS

### ANSWERS TO PRAYER

# *Day 293*

## GRACE AND PEACE

As you look around at God's blessings in your life, close your eyes and look inward as well. God has also provided you with an abundance of grace and peace. Grace that allows you to be who you genuinely are and the peace of knowing that who you are is just fine with Him.

*God, thank You for Your peace and grace. When I am tempted to become anxious about something, remind me that Your peace surrounds me. Give me a gentle nudge of assurance that Your grace is more than enough for me. I trust You.*

### PRAYER REQUESTS

### PRAISES

### ANSWERS TO PRAYER

# Day 294
## GET HAPPY!

We act as though comfort and luxury were the chief requirements of life,
when all we need to make us really happy is something to be enthusiastic about.
CHARLES KINGSLEY

⌇

*God! I am so excited about my relationship with You. It is something I will never
lose. You have promised that nothing can separate me from Your presence. I can
always have access to Your great love. I am filled with joy in just knowing You.*

........................................................................................
........................................................................................
........................................................................................
........................................................................................
........................................................................................
........................................................................................

### PRAISES

........................................
........................................
........................................
........................................
........................................
........................................
........................................
........................................
........................................
........................................

### PRAYER REQUESTS

........................................
........................................
........................................
........................................

### ANSWERS TO PRAYER

........................................
........................................
........................................
........................................

# ARE YOU READY?

God wants to bless you, and He will, but perhaps He has to get your attention first. As long as you're headed in the opposite direction, even if you received a blessing, you wouldn't appreciate it. Even the best God could give would become mired in your disobedience. God wants to bless you today. Are you ready to receive all the good He has to offer?

*God, thank You for pursuing me even when I go my own way. Forgive me when I've been rebellious toward You. Thank You for stopping me in my tracks and showing me the truth. I am ready to walk the path You've set before me. I choose You today.*

## PRAYER REQUESTS

## PRAISES

## ANSWERS TO PRAYER

## Day 296
# GOD'S GRACE

We know certainly that our God. . .gives us every grace,
every abundant grace; and though we are so weak of ourselves,
this grace is able to carry us through every obstacle and difficulty.
ELIZABETH ANN SETON

*God, grace flows from the very essence of who You are. I am so very thankful for Your*
*grace that You have provided to me. I choose to ride upon Your waves of grace in every*
*difficulty. May I remember Your grace in the midst of every trial and choose to rest in You.*

### PRAISES

### PRAYER REQUESTS

### ANSWERS TO PRAYER

# WISE REQUESTS

Give me work to do; give me health; give me joy in simple things. Give me an eye for beauty, a tongue for truth, a heart that loves. . . . And at the close of each day give me a book and a friend with whom I can be silent.

SCOTTIE MCKENZIE FRAZIER

*Lord, thank You for Your wisdom at work in my soul. In Your wisdom I ask for these things: work to do, health, joy in the simple things. Fill my spirit with Your wisdom so that I may choose each day to focus on the right things from You.*

## PRAYER REQUESTS

## PRAISES

## ANSWERS TO PRAYER

# BETWEEN HIS SHOULDERS

"Let the beloved of the LORD rest secure in him, for he shields him all day long, and the one the LORD loves rests between his shoulders. . . . May the LORD bless his land with the precious dew from heaven above and with the deep waters that lie below; with the best the sun brings forth and the finest the moon can yield."

DEUTERONOMY 33:12–14 NIV

*Lord, You are gracious, and I have no reason to fear anyone or anything. You are with me in all that I do. You bless the things I put my hand to. Help me to follow You all the days of my life, making wise choices that are in alignment with Your will for me.*

## PRAISES

## PRAYER REQUESTS

## ANSWERS TO PRAYER

# POSSIBILITIES = BLESSINGS

No matter how dark things seem to be or actually are, raise your sights
and see possibilities—always see them, for they're always there.

NORMAN VINCENT PEALE

*In the darkness, my heavenly Father, You are there. Sometimes I can't see You, but I am
not alone. I lift my eyes in anticipation of the light that I know will surely come to my situation. I am confident that You will bring about good things out of the darkest situations.*

## PRAYER REQUESTS

## PRAISES

## ANSWERS TO PRAYER

# *Day 300*
## PATIENT REVELATIONS

Our real blessings often appear to us in the shape of pains,
losses, and disappointments; but let us have patience and
we soon shall see them in their proper figures.
JOSEPH ADDISON

*Jesus, You said in this world I would have trouble but to have faith because You over-*
*came the world for me. As I look at the hard times, I will stand strong because You*
*are at my side. You have prepared me by Your grace to endure and see the victory.*

### PRAISES

### PRAYER REQUESTS

### ANSWERS TO PRAYER

## Day 301
# THE BEST ROAD MAP

God left us an owner's manual—the Bible. It's a road map
for life. In it, you'll discover the paths that lead to health,
wholeness, peace, renewed strength, and a beautiful life.

*Heavenly Father, I treasure Your Word. The scriptures help me to better understand*
*You, this world, and the one to come. It shows me how to live a life that pleases You. It*
*brings me closer to You and points me toward the future You have planned for my life.*

........................................................................................................................
........................................................................................................................
........................................................................................................................
........................................................................................................................
........................................................................................................................
........................................................................................................................

## PRAYER REQUESTS

........................................................
........................................................
........................................................
........................................................

## PRAISES

........................................................
........................................................
........................................................
........................................................
........................................................
........................................................
........................................................
........................................................
........................................................
........................................................
........................................................

## ANSWERS TO PRAYER

........................................................
........................................................
........................................................
........................................................

# Day 302
## SING AN ANGEL'S SONG

Kind words are the music of the world. They have a power
which seems to be beyond natural causes, as if they were some
angel's song which had lost its way and come on earth.

FREDERICK WILLIAM FABER

*You send Your Word into the world to save it. Your words are salvation and healing. Help me to also share words of hope and healing. May my words be music to the ears of a hurting world. May the songs of Your praise that pass my lips help others find their way to You.*

| PRAISES | PRAYER REQUESTS |
|---|---|
| | |
| | **ANSWERS TO PRAYER** |

# THE PRIVILEGE OF PRAYER

What a friend we have in Jesus,
All our sins and griefs to bear.
What a privilege to carry
Everything to God in prayer.
JOSEPH SCRIVEN

*What an honor to take everything to You in prayer, Jesus. You are my confidant, my friend, and my advocate. No one but You understands all that I deal with in this life. When I share my joys and sorrows, I know You get me like no one else does. Thank You for the privilege of prayer.*

## PRAYER REQUESTS

## PRAISES

## ANSWERS TO PRAYER

## Day 304

# INFINITELY BLESSED

And all these blessings shall come upon you and overtake you, because you obey the voice of the LORD your God: "Blessed shall you be in the city, and blessed shall you be in the country. . . . Blessed shall you be when you come in, and blessed shall you be when you go out."

DEUTERONOMY 28:2–3, 6 NKJV

*Thank You, Lord, for speaking to me. I tune my ears to hear Your voice. When You call to me, I respond in faith and obedience. Thank You for the blessings You freely give to me wherever I go. I am blessed every way I turn. Your goodness is my companion, and Your mercy follows after me.*

### PRAISES

### PRAYER REQUESTS

### ANSWERS TO PRAYER

## Day 305
# THE HAPPIEST MOMENTS

The happiest moments of my life have been the few
which I have passed at home in the bosom of my family.
THOMAS JEFFERSON

*God, thank You for the idea of family. I know it was Your idea because
You desired a family from the beginning. And I am forever grateful
to be one of Your children. May I be a blessing to the family You've
given me. Help me to show them by example how to follow You.*

........................................................................................................
........................................................................................................
........................................................................................................
........................................................................................................
........................................................................................................

### PRAYER REQUESTS

........................................................
........................................................
........................................................
........................................................

### PRAISES

........................................................
........................................................
........................................................
........................................................
........................................................
........................................................
........................................................
........................................................
........................................................

### ANSWERS TO PRAYER

........................................................
........................................................
........................................................

# Day 306
## SIZE DOESN'T MATTER

If you have a special need today, focus your full attention on the goodness and greatness of your Father rather than on the size of your need. Your need is so small compared to His ability to meet it.

~

*You are the only God, the one who does miracles for Your name's sake. Help me see You as bigger than anything that could ever stand in my way. You make my paths straight and make a way when I can't see one. But You do miracles and wonders. That's who You are.*

### PRAISES

### PRAYER REQUESTS

### ANSWERS TO PRAYER

# Day 307
## HAPPY COINCIDENCES

*Dear Lord, thank You for happy coincidences and days when things just seem to fall into place. Help me to always remember and recognize these moments as examples of Your awesome power working in my life. All credit goes to You for the good things that come my way. Remind me to look up and give You praise. You are always at work in my life. So often I don't see anything happening until Your miraculous wonders are revealed to me. Thank You for making all things work together for my good as You have promised.*

....................................................................................................................................

....................................................................................................................................

....................................................................................................................................

....................................................................................................................................

....................................................................................................................................

....................................................................................................................................

....................................................................................................................................

### PRAYER REQUESTS

....................................................................

....................................................................

....................................................................

....................................................................

### ANSWERS TO PRAYER

....................................................................

....................................................................

....................................................................

....................................................................

### PRAISES

....................................................................

....................................................................

....................................................................

....................................................................

....................................................................

....................................................................

....................................................................

....................................................................

....................................................................

....................................................................

....................................................................

# Day 308
## SALVATION

The gift of God is that you have been saved through faith. Neither this faith nor salvation is owing to any works you ever did, will do, or can do.

~~~

*God, I was broken, lost, and alone. I had nothing to give but my empty self. Thank You for coming into my life, filling me with Your great love and tremendous grace. I owe everything to You. I surrender my life to You. Please use me to bring glory to Your name.*

..........................................................................................................................................

..........................................................................................................................................

..........................................................................................................................................

..........................................................................................................................................

..........................................................................................................................................

..........................................................................................................................................

### PRAISES

......................................................

......................................................

......................................................

......................................................

......................................................

......................................................

......................................................

......................................................

### PRAYER REQUESTS

......................................................

......................................................

......................................................

......................................................

### ANSWERS TO PRAYER

......................................................

......................................................

......................................................

# *Day 309*
## USE YOUR GIFTS

Whosoever takes up the burden of his neighbor. . .and ministers
unto those in need out of the abundance of things he has received
. . .of God's bounty—this man. . .is an imitator of God.

EPISTLE TO DIOGNETUS

*God Almighty, give me opportunities to open my hands to give Your kindness, to lighten
the load of others, and to share the abundant blessings You've provided for me. And
when I have that chance, may I never take the credit but always point others to You.*

.......................................................................................................................................
.......................................................................................................................................
.......................................................................................................................................
.......................................................................................................................................
.......................................................................................................................................

### PRAYER REQUESTS

.........................................................................
.........................................................................
.........................................................................
.........................................................................

### PRAISES

.........................................................................
.........................................................................
.........................................................................
.........................................................................
.........................................................................
.........................................................................
.........................................................................

### ANSWERS TO PRAYER

.........................................................................
.........................................................................
.........................................................................
.........................................................................

# UNFATHOMABLE LOVE

Then Christ will make his home in your hearts as you trust in him.
Your roots will grow down into God's love and keep you strong.
And may you have the power to understand, as all God's people
should, how wide, how long, how high, and how deep his love is.
EPHESIANS 3:17–18 NLT

*God, I am digging deep and reaching for Your unconditional, never-ending love for me. Give me the ability to understand just how much You love me. I never want to take Your great gift for granted. Help me to share it with every person I can.*

## PRAISES

## PRAYER REQUESTS

## ANSWERS TO PRAYER

# Day 311

## HOME SWEET HOME

Oh Thou, who dwellest in so many homes, possess Thyself of this. . . . Bless the life that is sheltered here. Grant that trust and peace and comfort abide within, and that love and life and usefulness may go out from this home forever.

UNKNOWN

*Father, thank You for the home You have given me and for each one who resides within. I pray that each one goes out in faith and returns through the doors in safety and provision. May my home be filled with Your presence and peace. May all who enter experience You.*

### PRAYER REQUESTS

### PRAISES

### ANSWERS TO PRAYER

# Day 312
## HIDDEN IDEALS

God hides some ideal in every human soul. At some time in our life we
feel a trembling, fearful longing to do some good thing. Life finds its
noblest spring of excellence in this hidden impulse to do our best.

ROBERT COLLYER

*God, thank You for the passion and desire in my soul to do something good.
I know that comes from You. And because of who You are, You've also
placed the ability within me by Your power to do that very thing. Give me
the strength to do it and the faith to believe You will make it happen.*

## PRAISES

## PRAYER REQUESTS

## ANSWERS TO PRAYER

# SPONTANEOUS BLESSINGS

Some of the best things in your life will come to you because of planning.
But some. . .will also come without planning for them at all. That's what
makes life so much fun. It's a daily surprise, and you need to stride
into it with faith, even if you don't know where you're going.

*Father, thank You for the story of Abraham, a man who willingly followed You
in obedience even though he didn't know where he was going. May I also follow
You by faith when I don't have the details but know You are leading me.*

## PRAYER REQUESTS

## PRAISES

## ANSWERS TO PRAYER

## Day 314

# GLORIOUS PREPARATIONS

Eternity is the divine treasure house, and hope is the window,
by means of which mortals are permitted to see, as through
a glass darkly, the things which God is preparing.
WILLIAM MOUNTFORD

*God, I am so very excited for the things You are preparing for me. I have great
expectation and am filled with anticipation of all the good You will set before
me. I have high hopes of the future I have in You today and for all eternity.*

### PRAISES

### PRAYER REQUESTS

### ANSWERS TO PRAYER

# Day 315
## SEEDS OF PEACE

*Lord, thank You for blessing me with so many fruitful relationships. Even when I'm feeling down or stuck in a rut, You've always led me to a helping hand or an understanding shoulder to cry on. Thank You for cultivating a sense of joy in me when I'm around those I love. I ask that You'd use me to spread Your seeds of peace in their lives as well. Lord, I am so very grateful for the divine connections You have made for me throughout my life. I consider these people family. I am so thankful to have them to do life with. I appreciate that we share faith in You and can encourage one another as we journey together toward eternity with You.*

PRAYER REQUESTS

PRAISES

ANSWERS TO PRAYER

# THE BEST GIFT GIVER

"If you then, being evil, know how to give good gifts to your children, how much more will your Father who is in heaven give good things to those who ask Him!"
MATTHEW 7:11 NKJV

*God, thank You for being a good Father who sets the excellent example of how to give. Teach me to be generous to others, especially my children. Give me wisdom to know what is the best gift. Lead me and guide me in my generosity to others.*

## PRAISES

## PRAYER REQUESTS

## ANSWERS TO PRAYER

# *Day 317*
# ADVERSITY BEGETS BLESSINGS

If we had no winter, the spring would not be so pleasant: if we did not
sometimes taste of adversity, prosperity would not be so welcome.

ANNE BRADSTREET

*God, why is it that I appreciate the blessings You give more when I face adversity?*
*Help me to have a grateful heart in every season. When I am blessed, may I willingly*
*and cheerfully bless others. And when it's a hard season, help me be grateful and receive.*

## PRAYER REQUESTS

## PRAISES

## ANSWERS TO PRAYER

# Day 318
## ORDINARY THINGS

Ordinary things have a great power to reveal the mysterious
nearness of a caring, liberating God. . . . In what seems ordinary
and everyday there is always more than at first meets the eye.

CHARLES CUMMINGS

*God, give me a curiosity to look deeper into the ordinary things in life. You are an extraor-
dinary God, so I know there is more to what I see than at first glance. Open my eyes to
see You and the things you are doing behind the scenes to bring Your plan to fruition.*

......................................................................................................................................

......................................................................................................................................

......................................................................................................................................

......................................................................................................................................

......................................................................................................................................

### PRAISES

### PRAYER REQUESTS

### ANSWERS TO PRAYER

# Day 319

## MORE THAN WE CONSIDER

Our heavenly Father knows how to give the best—gifts that have no price.
A sunset filled with vibrant colors, a nighttime sky. . .sprinkled with glowing
stars, a drink of water that quenches thirst as no man-made beverage can.
God has given generously in many more ways than we often consider.

*God, Your wondrous majesty surrounds me. Creation is a gift of beauty
that speaks to Your miraculous wonder. Thank You for giving me priceless
gifts inside and outside. Fill me today with the living water that only a
relationship with You can provide. May I overflow with joy onto others.*

### PRAYER REQUESTS

### PRAISES

### ANSWERS TO PRAYER

## Day 320
# MANY GUISES

When troubles come and things go wrong
And days are cheerless and nights are long. . . .
We add to our worries by refusing to try
To look for the rainbow in an overcast sky,
And the blessings God sent in a darkened disguise
Our troubled hearts fail to recognize,
Not knowing God sent it not to distress us
But to strengthen our faith and redeem us and bless us.

HELEN STEINER RICE

*God, I will trust Your promise that You are*
*working all things to my good. You are my hope.*

---

### PRAISES

### PRAYER REQUESTS

### ANSWERS TO PRAYER

*Day 321*

# THANKFULNESS REMAINS

First among the things to be thankful for is a thankful spirit.
. . . Happy are they who possess this gift! Blessings may fail
and fortunes vary, but the thankful heart remains.

UNKNOWN

*Lord, I desire to reflect all Your characteristics in my life, but above all, I pray I will always demonstrate a spirit of gratitude. You have saved me from so many things. My salvation is more than looking toward eternity. You also save me in the here and now.*

## PRAYER REQUESTS

## PRAISES

## ANSWERS TO PRAYER

# Day 322
## THE GOOD LIFE

"They will be radiant because of the LORD's good gifts—the abundant crops of grain, new wine, and olive oil, and the healthy flocks and herds. Their life will be like a watered garden, and all their sorrows will be gone."

JEREMIAH 31:12 NLT

*Dear Lord, Your good gifts spring up in my life and fill me with great joy. I am blessed beyond measure. Thank You for filling me with joy everlasting. You break the hold that sorrow once had on me. I lift my voice in praise to You today!*

### PRAISES

### PRAYER REQUESTS

### ANSWERS TO PRAYER

## Day 323
# REAP IN ABUNDANCE

The world is sown with good; but unless I turn my glad thoughts into
practical living and till my own field, I cannot reap a kernel of the good.
HELEN KELLER

*Father, my good intentions do nothing for me or for the kingdom of God if I don't
take action. Thank You for inspiring me to do good and giving me the determina-
tion to act. When I see an opportunity to do good, I will not shrink from it.*

.................................................................................................................

.................................................................................................................

.................................................................................................................

.................................................................................................................

.................................................................................................................

.................................................................................................................

### PRAYER REQUESTS

.................................................................

.................................................................

.................................................................

.................................................................

### PRAISES

.................................................................

.................................................................

.................................................................

.................................................................

.................................................................

.................................................................

.................................................................

.................................................................

.................................................................

### ANSWERS TO PRAYER

.................................................................

.................................................................

.................................................................

.................................................................

# THE CHOICE IS YOURS

Between the house and the store there are little pockets of happiness.
A bird, a garden, a friend's greeting, a child's smile, a cat in the sunshine
needing a stroke. Recognize them or ignore them. It's always up to you.
PAM BROWN

*Forgive me for being so focused on myself that I've missed the small joys that You bring into my day. Today I will look up and take notice of the gifts You share with me. Help me to notice each one and tuck them into my heart to remember them.*

## PRAISES

## PRAYER REQUESTS

## ANSWERS TO PRAYER

# HEAVENLY TREASURES

Even the poorest people on earth can lay aside eternal blessings. That's because heavenly treasures have nothing to do with our legal tender—no government creates or backs it. God's riches are collected in a currency of the heart that consists of things like forgiveness, humility, and charitable deeds.

*God, You count Your wealth in souls. Help me to remember that the currency of heaven is not just the number who come into relationship with You but also how we treat one another. I want to be a reflection of You, willing to live to give as You do.*

## PRAYER REQUESTS

## PRAISES

## ANSWERS TO PRAYER

# Day 326
## GOD'S QUIET STREAM

I will take special notice of the good things when they come. I will fix my mind on what is pure and lovely and upright. . . . I will not worry but keep on producing a life that is a blessing for You and others. Let me take time often to come drink from your quiet stream. I thank You for it.

ANITA CORRINE DONIHUE

*Pour Your presence on me. Give me spiritual food that satisfies my soul. You lead me by still waters and give me living water. I am thankful for each blessing You give me. Help me to always be generous to share what You give me.*

PRAISES

PRAYER REQUESTS

ANSWERS TO PRAYER

# FOREVER GRATEFUL

The private and personal blessings we enjoy, the blessings of immunity, safeguard, liberty, and integrity, deserve the thanksgiving of a whole life.

JEREMY TAYLOR

*Holy God, thank You for the freedoms I have in Christ. You have placed me in this country, and I pray that You lead us and guide us, protect us, and keep us. Continue to work through our leaders. May they safeguard our liberties and operate in integrity.*

## PRAYER REQUESTS

## PRAISES

## ANSWERS TO PRAYER

# OUR REWARD

This is what I have seen to be good and right: to eat and to drink and be happy in all the work one does under the sun during the few years of his life which God has given him. For this is his reward. . . . This is the gift of God.

ECCLESIASTES 5:18–19 NLV

*Lord, You are faithful to me. You provide for me and open doors so that I can bless my family and others. Your provision sustains us. Help me to see the work You've given me to do as a gift from You. I set my heart on You so that I accomplish the tasks You set before me.*

## PRAISES

## PRAYER REQUESTS

## ANSWERS TO PRAYER

# SWEET GRATITUDE

As flowers carry dewdrops, trembling on the edges of the petals, and
ready to fall at the first waft of wind or brush of bird, so the heart should
carry its beaded words of thanksgiving; and at the first breath of heavenly
flavor, let down the shower, perfumed with the heart's gratitude.

HENRY WARD BEECHER

*God, today I give thanks to You for the sweet pleasures in my life—Your tender guid-*
*ance, Your voice that speaks to me, Your gentle presence, and Your powerfully awe-*
*some love. Without You, I am nothing. You give me purpose, peace, and significance.*

## PRAYER REQUESTS

## ANSWERS TO PRAYER

## PRAISES

# Day 330
## PASS NOTHING BY

Half the joy of life is in little things taken on the run. Let us run if we must. . .but let us keep our hearts young and our eyes open that nothing worth our while shall escape us. And everything is worth its while if we only grasp it and its significance.
CHARLES VICTOR CHERBULIEZ

*Lord, I am constantly moving. It's really hard for me to slow down and take in Your grace, but You have instructed me in Your Word to "be still" and know You. Remind me to stop and look to You. I take a deep breath now and listen to You.*

PRAISES

PRAYER REQUESTS

ANSWERS TO PRAYER

## Day 331

# A LITTLE EFFORT = BIG REWARDS

Sometimes God doesn't hand us our rewards—we have to find them. It's not that God is playing games with us. He just knows that a little effort on our part will make us appreciate our rewards all the more.

*Father, Your Word says You are a rewarder when I diligently seek You. Create in me a clean heart. May my motives to serve You be pure. I don't seek You to get from You but to experience Your presence in my life. Help me to appreciate all You give me with a thankful heart.*

### PRAYER REQUESTS

### PRAISES

### ANSWERS TO PRAYER

# GIVE THANKS FOR DIVERSITY

Appreciate the members of your family for who they are, even though their outlook or style may be miles different from yours. Rabbits don't fly. Eagles don't swim. Ducks look funny trying to climb. Squirrels don't have feathers. Stop comparing. There's plenty of room in the forest.

CHUCK SWINDOLL

*Heavenly Father, I love my family so much. Forgive me for the times I lose my patience with them. Give me Your compassion and grace to show them what they mean to me and how much I truly love them. May my words always be a blessing to them.*

## PRAISES

## PRAYER REQUESTS

## ANSWERS TO PRAYER

# Day 333

## THE SWEETEST JOY

Friendship is one of the sweetest joys of life: many spirits might have failed beneath the bitterness of trial if they had not found a friend.

CHARLES SPURGEON

*Thank You, God, for my friends. I can never have too many friends. Give me a heart that cherishes time with friends. Give me ears to hear and a desire to help others when they have a need. Thank You for the amazing friends who are always there for me for the difficult times.*

---

### PRAYER REQUESTS

### PRAISES

### ANSWERS TO PRAYER

# DELIVERANCE

Blessed is he who considers the poor; the LORD will deliver him in time of trouble. The LORD will preserve him and keep him alive, and he will be blessed on the earth; You will not deliver him to the will of his enemies.

PSALM 41:1–2 NKJV

*Lord, thank You for blessing me. May I never forget to share with others what You've given me. Remind me to be generous and to approach others with my hands wide open, willing to give because You have been so gracious and giving to me.*

........................................................................................................................................

........................................................................................................................................

........................................................................................................................................

........................................................................................................................................

........................................................................................................................................

## PRAISES

## PRAYER REQUESTS

## ANSWERS TO PRAYER

# Day 335

## GO FORWARD JOYOUSLY

A new life begins for us with every second. Let us go forward joyously
to meet it. We must press on, whether we will or no, and we shall walk
better with our eyes before us than with them ever cast behind.

JEROME K. JEROME

*Lord, I remember the past, only to rejoice in Your goodness. I will not remember the*
*failures and pains that have been forgiven and healed. When others tempt me to look*
*back with regret, I will press forward in my heart and mind. Thank You for my new life.*

### PRAYER REQUESTS

### PRAISES

### ANSWERS TO PRAYER

## Day 336
# GENTLE GUIDANCE

Father, I know You will provide what's best for me even if I don't understand at the time. Let me walk in faith, confident that You know my path better than I do. Amen.

*Even when I feel alone, I believe You are there. Your promise to always be with me cannot fail. I am confident that I will see Your purpose and plan come to fruition in my lifetime. I continue to walk in the light of Your Word each day. Guide me every step of the way.*

## PRAISES

## PRAYER REQUESTS

## ANSWERS TO PRAYER

# PERSONALIZED GIFTS

God gives each of us different lives and different blessings designed just for us. Those blessings provide goodness and mercy on earth and continued joy in heaven. There's no dissonance between our song here on earth and the one that will praise Jesus eternally.

*Today I lift up my voice to the heavens and praise You, God Almighty. You are gracious to me. I will sing Your praise all my days. Your goodness and mercy on earth fill me with great joy. I am grateful for Your design of my life and the joy set aside for me.*

## PRAYER REQUESTS

## PRAISES

## ANSWERS TO PRAYER

# Day 338

## GOODNESS MULTIPLIERS

True friendship multiplies the good in life and divides its evils. Strive to have friends, for life without friends is like life on a desert island. To find one real friend in a lifetime is good fortune; to keep him is a blessing.

BALTASAR GRACIÁN

*God, bless my friends today. Thank You for bringing each one of them into my life. You have woven a tapestry of relationship together. We need one another. I refuse to let envy, strife, or division come between us. Multiply our love for one another.*

......................................................................................................

......................................................................................................

......................................................................................................

......................................................................................................

......................................................................................................

### PRAISES

......................................................

......................................................

......................................................

......................................................

......................................................

......................................................

......................................................

......................................................

......................................................

### PRAYER REQUESTS

......................................................

......................................................

......................................................

......................................................

### ANSWERS TO PRAYER

......................................................

......................................................

......................................................

......................................................

# Day 339

## SATISFACTION

Sometimes your expectation for the blessings of God require you to press a little harder and stretch your faith a little farther to see the results you've asked God for. You can be sure all your effort will be rewarded.

~

*Today I refuse to quit. I will press a little harder and stretch my faith even far-ther than I ever have. You have promised, God, and Your love for me never fails. I will be patient and wait on Your timing. You have the best in store for me.*

### PRAYER REQUESTS

### PRAISES

### ANSWERS TO PRAYER

# OUR WATCHFUL KEEPER

For sunlit hours and visions clear, For all remembered faces dear. . .
For friends who shared the year's long road, And bore with us the common load. . .
For insights won through toil and tears, We thank the Keeper of our years.

CLYDE McGEE

*Lord, You are my keeper. You lead me in blessing and favor. You've been with me
from day one. You will never lead me astray or remove me from Your hand. I lean
into You with all that I am. I trust You to live in me and through me all my days.*

......................................................................................................................................
......................................................................................................................................
......................................................................................................................................
......................................................................................................................................

## PRAISES

......................................................
......................................................
......................................................
......................................................
......................................................
......................................................
......................................................
......................................................
......................................................

## PRAYER REQUESTS

......................................................
......................................................
......................................................
......................................................

## ANSWERS TO PRAYER

......................................................
......................................................
......................................................

# BE A BLESSING

Everyone you meet is fighting some kind of battle, and your smile, your kind word, your hand of friendship will make a difference in their day and will change how they see things. You can be the change. You can bless those around you.

KAREN MOORE

*Help me, Jesus, to be a difference maker. Help me to see the hurt others feel. Give me words of love and blessing that show them You see and love them. I want to be the change that points them to You.*

PRAYER REQUESTS

PRAISES

ANSWERS TO PRAYER

# Day 342
## GOOD WISHES

May God give you. . .for every storm, a rainbow; for every tear, a smile; for every care, a promise; and a blessing in each trial. For every problem life sends, a faithful friend to share; for every sigh, a sweet song; and an answer for each prayer.

IRISH BLESSING

*Thank You, Father, for Your plans for me. You have prepared a future for me filled with good things. I trust and believe good things are to come. I have an excitement and expectation for Your good at work in my life. I walk in the blessings You set before me.*

........................................................................................

........................................................................................

........................................................................................

........................................................................................

| PRAISES | PRAYER REQUESTS |
|---------|-----------------|
|         |                 |
|         | **ANSWERS TO PRAYER** |
|         |                 |

## Day 343

# SHARE THE NEWS!

God has wonderful gifts in mind for you. If you ask, He'll show
you what gifts He's given you and how He wants you to impact
others with them. Don't wait until eternity to experience the joys
and delights of faith—share some of that good news today!

*God, sometimes it's easier not to share. People are unpredictable. It's risky
to share my gifts for fear of judgment or rejection. Help me to embrace
the moment and share without concern about how people will respond or
caring what they think. I choose to be obedient and filled with faith.*

.............................................................................................................................
.............................................................................................................................
.............................................................................................................................
.............................................................................................................................
.............................................................................................................................

## PRAYER REQUESTS

.....................................................................
.....................................................................
.....................................................................
.....................................................................

## ANSWERS TO PRAYER

.....................................................................
.....................................................................
.....................................................................
.....................................................................

## PRAISES

.....................................................................
.....................................................................
.....................................................................
.....................................................................
.....................................................................
.....................................................................
.....................................................................
.....................................................................
.....................................................................
.....................................................................
.....................................................................
.....................................................................

# Day 344
## TWO WAYS TO LIVE

There are only two ways to live your life. One is as though nothing
is a miracle. The other is as though everything is a miracle.

ALBERT EINSTEIN

*Lord, help me to see the miracles You perform in my life and in the lives of those around
me. I don't want to miss a thing. I delight in Your presence and love to see Your majesty
unfold. Each day is a gift You open before me, presenting it with love and tenderness.*

PRAISES

PRAYER REQUESTS

ANSWERS TO PRAYER

# *Day 345*

# HIDDEN REWARDS

*Oh Lord, You care for every part of my life and know me inside out. Although some of my rewards may be hidden right now, I am confident You will help me find them. I love the unexpected, undeserved treasures You hide for me to find. You know what I need before I even ask. And when I don't know what I want, You reward me with gifts I never even imagined. You are a good Father. I love You!*

## PRAYER REQUESTS

## PRAISES

## ANSWERS TO PRAYER

# Day 346

## A FEAST OF GIFTS

"The young women will dance for joy, and the men—old and young—
will join in the celebration. I will turn their mourning into joy. I will
comfort them and exchange their sorrow for rejoicing. The priests will
enjoy abundance, and my people will feast on my good gifts."

JEREMIAH 31:13–14 NLT

*Terrible things happen in this fallen world. When my heart hurts, I run to You. When I
grieve, I give You my broken heart. Each time, You take it and restore my joy. You comfort
me and show me how to live one day at a time, accepting the good gifts You offer me.*

.........................................................................................................................

.........................................................................................................................

.........................................................................................................................

.........................................................................................................................

.........................................................................................................................

### PRAISES

### PRAYER REQUESTS

### ANSWERS TO PRAYER

# Day 347

## MIRACLES

To be alive, to be able to see, to walk, to have a home—it's all a miracle.
I have adopted the technique of living life from miracle to miracle.

ARTHUR RUBINSTEIN

*Miracles happen every day, even when we don't see them. You take me from miracle to miracle. I could have fallen. I should have died. And yet You keep me safe. You stretch out a net before me and keep me secure. Thank You for being the God of miracles in my life.*

### PRAYER REQUESTS

### ANSWERS TO PRAYER

### PRAISES

# GOD'S KEEPING

To be in God's keeping is surely a blessing,
For though life is often dark and distressing,
No day is too dark and no burden too great
That God in His love cannot penetrate.

HELEN STEINER RICE

*Each day You keep me in all my ways. Each night You bless me with sweet peace.*
*Thank You for Your great love. Nothing can remove me from Your hand. No matter*
*what I face, You are with me, comforting me and giving me strength for another day.*

## PRAISES

## PRAYER REQUESTS

## ANSWERS TO PRAYER

# Day 349
## JOYOUS SOUNDS

May none of God's wonderful works keep silence, night or morning.
Bright stars, high mountains, the depths of the seas, sources of rushing rivers:
may all these break into song as we sing to the Father, Son, and Holy Spirit.
UNKNOWN

*Let the heavens declare Your glory, God, and the skies show the work of
Your hands. Each time I open my mouth or think things of my heart, I want
to please You. I desire for all I say and do to agree with Your ways.*

### PRAYER REQUESTS

### PRAISES

### ANSWERS TO PRAYER

# Day 350
## ETERNAL THANKS

Now thank we all our God, with heart and hands and voices,
Who wondrous things hath done, in whom His world rejoices;
Who from our mothers' arms, hath blessed us on our way
With countless gifts of love, and still is ours today.

MARTIN RINKART

*I owe my life to You, God. All I am, all I have, only exists because of Your matchless love for me. I rejoice today because You loved me first and called me as Your own by faith before the world was made. I lift my voice in praise to You, Almighty God.*

## PRAISES

## PRAYER REQUESTS

## ANSWERS TO PRAYER

## *Day 351*
# TRUE CONTENTMENT

We tend to forget that happiness doesn't come as a result of getting something we don't have, but rather of recognizing and appreciating what we do have.
FRIEDRICH KOENIG

*Lord, let Your light shine in me today. May I be content with every gift You've given me. You are good, and Your goodness is present in my life. Thank You for unspeakable joy that only comes from You. Show me how to share it best with the rest of the world.*

........................................................................................................
........................................................................................................
........................................................................................................
........................................................................................................
........................................................................................................
........................................................................................................

### PRAYER REQUESTS

### PRAISES

### ANSWERS TO PRAYER

# Day 352

## HOLIDAY GIFTS

You make known to me the path of life; you will fill me with joy
in your presence, with eternal pleasures at your right hand.

PSALM 16:11 NIV

*My mind cannot fathom the pleasures of heaven that await me. I can only imagine the tremendous love You have shown me here on earth will be multiplied on a heavenly scale. Thank You for the joy You give me. Thank You for Your presence here and now.*

### PRAISES

### PRAYER REQUESTS

### ANSWERS TO PRAYER

## Day 353

# THE MIRACLE OF KINDNESS

This is the miracle that happens every time to those who
really love: the more they give, the more they possess.

RAINER MARIA RILKE

*Father, I am always so surprised when people comment about the kindness shown them
or the love expressed to them. It seems like they never expect it, and yet it is who You
are. The more I come to know You, the more I desire to express Your love to others.*

...............................................................................................................................

...............................................................................................................................

...............................................................................................................................

...............................................................................................................................

...............................................................................................................................

...............................................................................................................................

...............................................................................................................................

### PRAYER REQUESTS

..........................................................................

..........................................................................

..........................................................................

..........................................................................

### ANSWERS TO PRAYER

..........................................................................

..........................................................................

..........................................................................

..........................................................................

### PRAISES

..........................................................................

..........................................................................

..........................................................................

..........................................................................

..........................................................................

..........................................................................

..........................................................................

..........................................................................

..........................................................................

..........................................................................

..........................................................................

..........................................................................

..........................................................................

..........................................................................

# THE BEAUTY UNDERNEATH

Life is so full of meaning and purpose, so full of beauty beneath
its covering, that you will find earth but cloaks your heaven.

FRA GIOVANNI

~

*Dear God, the deeper I go and the more I grow in knowing You, the more beautiful You are to me. I desire to be filled with Your presence. I want to experience You on a deeper level. Thank You for showing Yourself to me in new ways.*

......................................................................................................................

......................................................................................................................

......................................................................................................................

......................................................................................................................

......................................................................................................................

......................................................................................................................

## PRAISES

......................................................

......................................................

......................................................

......................................................

......................................................

......................................................

......................................................

......................................................

......................................................

## PRAYER REQUESTS

......................................................

......................................................

......................................................

......................................................

## ANSWERS TO PRAYER

......................................................

......................................................

......................................................

......................................................

# *Day 355*
## SPIRITUAL FILL-UP

What a blessing, to continually receive more and more of God's mercy, peace, and love. God gives blessings so we can encourage, teach, and lead others into a relationship with Him. If we receive God's gifts and pass them on to others, God fills us again.

*I am finding more and more that I am never completely empty. The more I pour out of my spirit, the more I hunger for You. As I continue to give out, You fill me right back up so that I can continue to give and receive portions of You.*

### PRAYER REQUESTS

### PRAISES

### ANSWERS TO PRAYER

# Day 356
## DAILY TREASURES

Dear Jesus, help me not to be so busy that I miss the small pleasures You've sprinkled through my day. Help me notice the way the sunlight flickers through the leaves outside my kitchen window; help me pay attention to the smile of sympathy my coworker gives me. I thank you for all your gifts, seen and unseen. Amen.

ELLYN SANNA

*No, don't let me miss a single thing. Your gifts are innumerable and Your miracles beyond my understanding. But they are to be experienced and cherished. Help me to see You even in the simplest parts of my day.*

### PRAISES

### PRAYER REQUESTS

### ANSWERS TO PRAYER

# Day 357

## QUIET BLESSINGS

How silently, how silently,
The wondrous gift is given!
So God imparts to human hearts
The blessings of His heaven.

PHILLIPS BROOKS

*I close my eyes in prayer right now, waiting to spend time with You. Thank You for meeting me where I am. You are always ready to impart a calm assurance to my heart. In the quiet I ask, and You always answer. Thank You for always being there for me.*

### PRAYER REQUESTS

### PRAISES

### ANSWERS TO PRAYER

# THE ULTIMATE GIFT

But when the right time came, God sent his Son, born of a woman,
subject to the law. God sent him to buy freedom for us who were slaves
to the law, so that he could adopt us as his very own children.

GALATIANS 4:4–5 NLT

*Jesus, thank You for leaving heaven and coming to die for me. Thank You for exchanging all that You had as the Son of God so that I could become a child of God and live eternally in Your family. It was a gift only You could give, and I am grateful!*

## PRAISES

## PRAYER REQUESTS

## ANSWERS TO PRAYER

# A REASON TO REJOICE

'Twas a humble birthplace, but O how much God gave to us that day,
From the manger bed what a path has led, What a perfect, holy way.
Alleluia! O how the angels sang. Alleluia! How it rang! And the sky
was bright with a holy light. 'Twas the birthday of a king.

WILLIAM H. NEIDLINGER

*The thought of baby Jesus is a sweet scene, but the reality of my redemption is the real picture of why He came. Thank You, Jesus, for Your willingness to bleed and die. Thank You for taking my place so that I could have eternal life.*

## PRAYER REQUESTS

## PRAISES

## ANSWERS TO PRAYER

# WHATEVER IS BEST

And always God's ready and eager and willing
To pour out His mercy, completely fulfilling
All of man's needs for peace, joy, and rest,
For God gives His children whatever is best.
Just give Him a chance to open His treasures,
And He'll fill your life with unfathomable pleasures.

HELEN STEINER RICE

*Thank You for Your Word. It is a treasure chest of Your goodness. It brings me answers to my questions. It shows me who You are and who You created me to be. It is truth that comes alive and lives in me. Thank You for always giving me Your very best.*

## PRAISES

## PRAYER REQUESTS

## ANSWERS TO PRAYER

## Day 361
# GIVE AND RECEIVE

God offers this wonderful blessing: those who give will also receive.
Whether it's money, time, energy, or another commodity, spiritual
or physical, God does not forget anything we've done. He never
ignores any generous gifts we offer at a price to ourselves.

*Lord, when You prompt my heart to give, help me to be a cheerful, prompt giver. I
never want to hold anything back from You. When You direct me to give, I know it is
for my good. As I cast my bread upon the water, it comes back to me on every wave.*

## PRAYER REQUESTS

## PRAISES

## ANSWERS TO PRAYER

# Day 362
## UNDER HIS WING

Look back through all your experiences, and think of the ways that the Lord your God has led you and how He has fed and clothed you every day.

*From the beginning, Lord, You have never failed me. You have always taken care of me. You have always made a way when I couldn't see the way. As I remember Your never-failing provision, I grow in my trust, knowing You will continue to care for me.*

.................................................................................................................

.................................................................................................................

.................................................................................................................

.................................................................................................................

.................................................................................................................

.................................................................................................................

.................................................................................................................

### PRAISES

.....................................................
.....................................................
.....................................................
.....................................................
.....................................................
.....................................................
.....................................................
.....................................................
.....................................................

### PRAYER REQUESTS

.....................................................
.....................................................
.....................................................
.....................................................

### ANSWERS TO PRAYER

.....................................................
.....................................................
.....................................................
.....................................................

# A LIMITLESS SUPPLY

You can trust God right now to supply all your needs for today. And if
your needs are more tomorrow, His supply will be greater also.

UNKNOWN

*Forgive me when I worry about tomorrow. I have what I need today, and that should
be enough. It doesn't matter how You'll work it out. You have promised never to fail
me, never to give up on me. And that is enough. Today I hold on to hope and believe.*

## PRAYER REQUESTS

## PRAISES

## ANSWERS TO PRAYER

# Day 364

## UNWAVERING FAITH

We are ignored, even though we are well known. We live close to death,
but we are still alive. We have been beaten, but we have not been killed.
Our hearts ache, but we always have joy. We are poor, but we give spiritual
riches to others. We own nothing, and yet we have everything.

2 CORINTHIANS 6:9–10 NLT

*I wish I had rock-solid faith. But I do falter and doubt sometimes. Still, I grow each
time my belief system is challenged. I want to say yes, God will, without a doubt.
I am growing stronger. I can stand a little longer. Lord, increase my faith.*

### PRAISES

### PRAYER REQUESTS

### ANSWERS TO PRAYER

## *Day 365*
# FUTURE BLESSINGS

God has seasons in our lives. . . . He is creating something you'll enjoy
in the future. You may not understand it today, but a month or year later,
you'll experience the benefits of new growth He was watering.

*Thank You for being present in my past, staying with me in the present, and going
ahead of me in the future. Your omnipresence, God, is one of the things about You
that is so mysterious to me, but I take great comfort in knowing You ARE.*

## PRAYER REQUESTS

## PRAISES

## ANSWERS TO PRAYER

# NOTES

# NOTES

# NOTES

# NOTES

# NOTES

# NOTES

# NOTES

# NOTES

# NOTES

# NOTES

# NOTES

# NOTES

# NOTES